P9-ELT-414

The Cupcake Bible

Publications International, Ltd.

Louis Weber, CEO
Publications International, Ltd.
7373 North Cicero Avenue
Lincolnwood, IL 60712

Some of the products listed in this publication may be in limited distribution.

Recipe development on pages 150 and 206 by Carissa Kinyon.

Recipe development on pages 22, 114, 134, 140, 188, 192, 200, 208, 210, 218, 228 and 242 by Jamie Schleser.

Recipe development on pages 16, 42, 66, 78, 212 and 216 by Ruth Siegel.

Recipe development on pages 48, 56, 132, 142, 144, 194, 214, 224, 232, 236 and 240 by Lauren Smekhov.

Recipe development on page 220 by Jennifer Worrell.

Front cover photography (bottom) and photography on pages 17, 23, 25, 43, 49, 57, 67, 77, 79, 81, 85, 87, 113, 115, 127, 133, 135, 141, 143, 145, 149, 151, 155, 181, 189, 193, 195, 201, 207, 209, 211, 213, 215, 217, 219, 221, 225, 229, 233, 237, 241 and 243 by PIL Photo Studio, Chicago.

Photographer: Tate Hunt
Photographer's Assistant: Justin Paris
Prop Stylist: Thomas Hamilton
Food Stylists: Kim Hartman, Mary Ann Melone, Kathy Joy, Carol Smoler
Assistant Food Stylists: Elaine Funk, Sheila Grannen, Lissa Levy, Breana Moeller

Pictured on the front cover *(clockwise from top):* Lemon Poppy Seed Cupcakes *(page 224),* Classic Chocolate Cupcakes *(page 70),* Pistachio-Chocolate Chip Cupcakes *(page 140),* Strawberry Milkshake Cupcakes *(page 22),* Classic Chocolate Cupcakes *(page 70)* and Margarita Cupcakes *(page 74).*
Pictured on the back cover *(clockwise from top):* Dark Chocolate Banana Cupcakes *(page 150),* Blueberry Cupcakes with Goat Cheese Frosting *(page 224)* and Mini Bees *(page 42).*

Photography on pages 5, 6, 7, 8, 9, 10, 11 and 12 by Shutterstock.
Photography on pages 11 and 12 by MediaBakery.

ISBN-13: 978-1-4508-1099-9
ISBN-10: 1-4508-1099-3

Library of Congress Control Number: 2010938751

Manufactured in China.

8 7 6 5 4 3 2 1

Microwave Cooking: Microwave ovens vary in wattage. Use the cooking times as guidelines and check for doneness before adding more time.

Preparation/Cooking Times: Preparation times are based on the approximate amount of time required to assemble the recipe before cooking, baking, chilling or serving. These times include preparation steps such as measuring, chopping and mixing. The fact that some preparations and cooking can be done simultaneously is taken into account. Preparation of optional ingredients and serving suggestions is not included.

Publications International, Ltd.

Table of Contents

Introduction 4

Spring Celebrations 16

Summer Sunshine 46

Fall Flavors 76

Winter Wonderland 114

Chocolate Overload 150

Just for Giggles 188

All Dressed Up 220

Acknowledgments 246

Index 247

Introduction

Cupcake Fundamentals

Playful, personal and portable, cupcakes are the perfect treat for every occasion. While you can find cupcakes almost everywhere you go today, homemade sweets always taste better and baking them couldn't be easier. Whether you are a novice or an expert in the kitchen, *The Cupcake Bible* will help you create beautiful cupcakes that will have your friends and family in awe. Beginners will appreciate recipes that start with a no-fail cake mix and offer options for simply spreading on frosting, making it as easy as possible to create delicious results. More experienced bakers will find exciting new flavors of cupcakes to make from scratch and will be inspired by the dazzling photography to push their decorating skills to new heights.

In this first section, you'll find everything you need to know to be successful: tips and tricks for improving your baking technique, information on necessary tools and equipment, and a helpful guide to substitutions should you be unable to find a particular ingredient or run out of something at the last second. It may look like a lot of information, but don't be overwhelmed. As you read through, you'll be pleasantly surprised to find that baking isn't as scary as it might seem. Good sense and good habits go a long way. In fact, baking is the easy part! Decorating is often much more challenging if you don't have a lot of experience with piping bags and candy sprinkles, but even that gets easier with practice. Don't be afraid to just grab an apron, embrace your inner cupcake goddess, and dive into the kitchen.

Homemade Treats

Many of the recipes in this collection, particularly those that call for more intricate decorations, begin with cupcakes made from a store-bought cake mix. Feel free to substitute your favorite basic cupcake recipe. Just prepare and bake the same amount of undecorated cupcakes, then follow the directions for frosting and finishing them.

Tangy Raspberry Minis, pg. 56

Beyond the introduction, you'll find an unparalleled collection of irresistible cupcake recipes. Seasonal chapters offer possibilities for every day of the year, including holidays, with lighter, brighter flavors for spring and summer and richer, soul-satisfying options for winter and fall. Chocolate lovers will relish in an entire chapter dripping with a rainbow of bittersweet, semisweet, milk and white chocolate. Kids will love the magical world of animals, hidden treats and wild colors that come to life in cupcake form, while adults will appreciate the refined sophistication of cupcakes transformed into tiny layer cakes or infused with grown-up flavor combinations like the creamy tartness of blueberries and goat cheese or the salty sweetness of maple syrup and bacon.

Maple Bacon Cupcakes, pg. 232

Getting Started

Picture-perfect cupcakes start with good baking habits. Keep the following techniques in mind every time the cupcake craving hits.

- Read the entire recipe before beginning to make sure you have all the necessary ingredients, utensils and supplies.
- For the best results, use the ingredients called for in the recipe.
- Remove butter, margarine and/or cream cheese from the refrigerator to soften, if necessary. Be aware that the amount of time it takes for these ingredients to reach the ideal consistency will be much shorter when the weather outside is hot and humid.

- Measure all of the ingredients accurately and assemble them in the order they are called for in the recipe. This is essential since combining certain ingredients too soon can cause unwanted results. Letting batter sit too long before baking can cause gluten in the flour to overdevelop, resulting in cupcakes that are tough instead of tender. It can also cause leavening agents to activate too soon, leaving the finished cupcakes with flat or even sunken tops.

- Complete any prep work—such as toasting or chopping nuts, peeling and slicing fruit, or melting chocolate or butter—before actually beginning to make the recipe so that you can complete every step as directed.
- Use the muffin cup size that is specified in the recipe or the yield and the baking time will not be accurate.
- Adjust the oven racks and then preheat the oven. Allow about 15 minutes for the oven to come up to temperature. Check the oven temperature for accuracy with an oven thermometer.
- Follow recipe directions and baking times exactly. Check for doneness using the test given in the recipe. Begin testing a few minutes before the end of the specified baking time.
- If you are placing more than one muffin pan in the oven at a time, make sure that the oven racks are evenly spaced and stagger the pans so that they are not directly over each other. If the distribution of heat in your oven is uneven, it may also be helpful to rotate the pans once during baking, moving the pan on the top rack to the bottom rack and vice versa.
- Avoid opening the oven during the first half of the baking time. The oven temperature needs to remain as constant as possible in order for the cupcakes to rise properly.
- It is best to have enough muffin pans to make the entire recipe at once; however, if you must reuse the same pans, make sure to cool them completely before filling them again. To expedite the process, heavy metal muffin pans should be allowed to cool slightly, then rinsed under cool water. Wiped dry, they will be ready to go again in no time.

Equipment

Having the right equipment is essential for any baking project. Fortunately, you probably already have most of the necessary tools for creating cupcake masterpieces at home in your kitchen. If not, make sure that you purchase the best quality that you can afford when shopping for new pieces—these items may cost a little more, but they are worth the investment since they will produce better results and last longer. Heavy metal muffin pans will stand up better to repeated washings and resist warping far longer than thinner pans that may only be a few dollars less, so choose wisely.

Baking Cups

Baking cups are used to line the cavities in a muffin pan. Made from paper or foil, they prevent cupcakes from sticking to the pan and make them easy to handle and transport. Though originally designed to be functional, baking cups can also add an element of decoration to the finished cupcakes. Grocery stores may only have one or two varieties available, usually in solid colors, but craft stores typically provide more options. Online baking supply stores offer savvy shoppers a seemingly limitless array of colorful designs in all different sizes, including baking cups designed specifically for seasonal use and special occasions, delicate paper sleeves that can be placed over plain baking cups, and cups made from waxed paper which help keep cupcakes moist during storage.

Cooling Racks

A cooling rack is a raised wire rack used to cool baked goods. It is raised to allow air circulation around the baked goods or baking pan, which speeds cooling and prevents steam accumulation that results in soggy treats. Choose stable racks that are at least ½ inch high for good circulation, with the metal wires close together so that even mini cupcakes sit squarely on them without tipping over. Another option is a wire mesh rack (with small square grids) that provides more support and will eliminate any instability. Cooling racks come in various sizes and are often included when purchasing a set of baking pans.

Decorating Bags

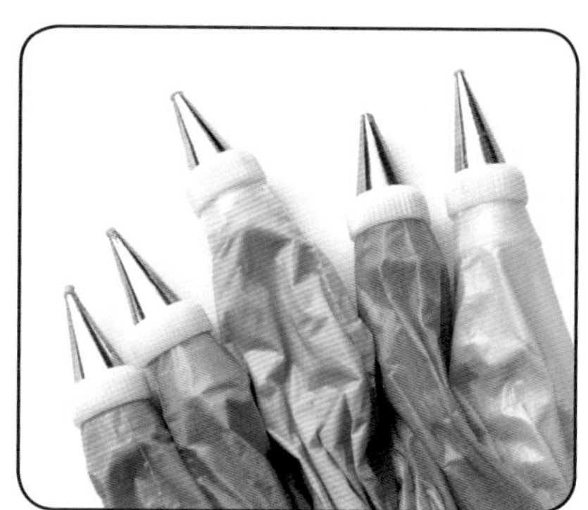

A decorating bag, also called a pastry bag, is a cone-shaped bag made of canvas, plastic or plastic-lined cloth. It is used to pipe foods, such as frosting, whipped cream or dough in a decorative pattern. It is open at both ends. The food to be piped is placed in the larger opening, while the smaller opening is fitted with decorative tips made of plastic or metal. (A small resealable plastic food storage bag with a tiny hole cut from the corner of the bag can also take the place of a pastry bag for simple decorating.) A quick alternative to a pastry bag for decorating baked goods is a plastic squeeze bottle—filled with melted chocolate or icing, it can make drizzling and decorating easier, especially for the novice.

Electric Mixers

An electric mixer is not essential, but if you bake often, it does make the process quicker and easier. Stand mixers are a significant investment, but they can handle larger quantities of dough and mixtures that are more dense thanks to a solid base, a heavy-duty motor and several adjustable speeds. Hand-held mixers have two removable beaters attached to plastic or metal housing that holds the mixer's motor. They can do most of the operations of stand mixers and offer the convenience of portability, but they sometimes have difficulty with heavy doughs. (They also leave you with only one free hand.)

Food Processors

A food processor can be used for mixing doughs and batters, but it is not always the best tool for this job. Its ability to produce a good end result will depend on the age and capacity of the machine, the size of the motor and the sharpness of the blade; you should consult the manufacturer's directions for making dough in the food processor. It does chop, slice, shred and purée very well, however, and in a fraction of the time it takes to do them by hand.

Graters

A four-sided box grater is a versatile and inexpensive tool with openings on each side sized to produce a different result; it can be used for grating citrus peel and chocolate in addition to its more common functions, grating cheese and vegetables. Smaller graters with handles may be less versatile but can perform all the same functions and may be easier to use and more convenient for baking jobs—these can be kept in a drawer or hung on a hook with other utensils.

Knives

Good-quality knives are important in baking as well as cooking, but only a few of them are used with regularity. A chef's knife has a wide, slightly curved blade from 7 to 12 inches long; it is used for most chopping tasks (such as nuts, dried fruit or chocolate). A paring knife has a short 2- to 3-inch-long blade and is used for peeling and slicing fruit, cutting out garnishes and other small jobs. A serrated knife is useful for trimming or slicing cupcakes for more fanciful presentations.

Measuring Cups

All bakers need two types of measuring cups. Dry measuring cups are used for ingredients such as sugar and flour, as well as for solid shortening. They come in sets of nested and graduated cups made of metal or plastic, including ¼ cup, ⅓ cup, ½ cup and 1 cup measures. (Some sets may include ⅛ cup, ⅔ cup and ¾ cup as well.) Dry measuring cups do not measure liquids accurately.

Liquid measuring cups are, as the name implies, just for measuring liquids. They are available in glass, plastic and metal, but clear glass is the most practical choice—you can see the liquid you are measuring and it is a heatproof material, making it ideal for portioning hot liquids or even melting chocolate in the microwave. Liquid measuring cups have calibrations marked on the side, a small pouring spout and a handle opposite the spout. You should look for a set that includes 1-cup, 2-cup and 4-cup sizes.

Introduction

When preparing a recipe, always use standardized measuring spoons and cups. For dry ingredients, fill the appropriate measuring spoon or cup to overflowing and level it off with a metal spatula or the flat edge of a knife. When measuring flour, lightly spoon it into the measuring cup, then level it off. Do not tap or bang the measuring cup since this will pack the flour. If a recipe calls for "sifted flour," sift the flour before it is measured. If a recipe calls for "flour, sifted," measure the flour first and then sift.

For liquid ingredients, place the cup on a flat surface, fill to the desired mark and check the measurement at eye level. To make sure that sticky liquids, such as corn syrup, honey and molasses, won't cling to the measuring cup, lightly grease the cup with vegetable oil or nonstick cooking spray first before filling it. Liquid measuring cups cannot be used to measure dry ingredients.

Cake Mix You Can Count On

If you're in a hurry, a cake mix is an easy way to make about 24 standard (2½-inch) cupcakes or 60 mini (1¾-inch) cupcakes. Just follow the directions on the package and you'll have blank cupcake canvases ready for decorating in no time.

Measuring Spoons

Measuring spoons come in nested sets of ¼ teaspoon, ½ teaspoon, 1 teaspoon and 1 tablespoon. (Some sets also include ⅛ teaspoon and 1½ teaspoons.) Available in metal or plastic, measuring spoons are used to measure small amounts of either dry or liquid ingredients. Do not substitute the teaspoons and tablespoons from your everyday flatware to measure ingredients; these spoons don't hold the same amount as measuring spoons.

Muffin Pans

Muffins pans are rectangular baking pans with 6, 12 or even 24 cup-shaped cavities. A standard muffin cup measures 2½ inches in diameter and is 1½ inches deep. Also available are jumbo muffin pans with cups that are 3¼ inches in diameter and 2 inches deep and mini pans with cups that are 1½ to 2 inches in diameter and ¾ inch deep. Traditional muffin pans are made of aluminum, steel or cast iron. New options made from silicone are becoming popular today and are typically available either as a multi-cup pan or single cups. Silicone stands up beautifully to the high heat of the oven and the flexibleness of the material makes it easier to remove the baked cupcakes; however, they often need to be placed on a sheet pan for support. If you are considering silicone muffin pans, you should also take into account that silicone does not conduct heat as well as metal so it may take longer for the cupcakes to bake and the finished treats may not have the same lovely golden brown color.

Oven Thermometer

Actual oven temperatures frequently vary quite a bit from the dial setting, so it is essential to keep a good-quality mercury oven thermometer in your oven all the time and adjust the dial setting to compensate as necessary. Most home ovens are off between 5 and 50 degrees, and sometimes even more. If your oven temperature isn't correct, your baked goods will be underbaked or overbaked.

Scoops

Stainless steel ice cream scoops with squeeze handles are used not only for portioning ice cream but also for portioning cookie dough or other batters. They are ideal for creating perfectly uniform cupcakes (which can be difficult to do using a spoon or pouring freehand). Scoops come in a variety of sizes and are labeled with a number from 8 to 100—the smaller the number, the larger the bowl of the scoop. (This number indicates the number of scoops that can be made from one quart of ice cream.) When shopping online, you may also find scoops listed by their diameter or capacity. For portioning standard cupcakes, you should look for a scoop that holds about 3 to 4 tablespoons of batter.

Sifter

A flour sifter consists of a fine mesh screen and a mechanism to push flour through the mesh. Sifting aerates dry ingredients such as flour, powdered sugar and cocoa powder; it also breaks up lumps and gives dry mixtures a uniform consistency. A sifter with a 2- to 3-cup capacity is a good choice, but you can also use fine mesh strainer, tapping on the lip of strainer to move the dry ingredients through. Never wash a sifter; just wipe it out with a damp paper towel.

Spatulas

Rubber spatulas, sometimes called scrapers, are flexible utensils with a paddlelike rubber, plastic or nylon head attached to a handle. They come in a wide variety of sizes and are ideal for scraping out the insides of bowls, containers and measuring cups. The larger ones are also good for blending dough and folding delicate mixtures together. Some of the newer rubber spatulas are heatproof; however, they are not as flexible as regular rubber spatulas.

Narrow metal spatulas have flexible metal blades attached to plastic or wooden handles. They are useful for leveling off dry ingredients when measuring and are ideal for spreading batters and frostings. While longer versions are ideal for baking and decorating layer cakes, you should choose one with a 3- or 4-inch blade for working with cupcakes. A flat spatula forms a straight line from handle to blade. An offset spatula is angled near the handle, causing the handle to be raised slightly.

Timer

A timer is extremely helpful when baking cupcakes, as a minute or two can mean the difference between moist, tender results and a dry, crumbly disaster. Many ranges, ovens and microwave ovens have built-in timers that can do the job. Free-standing timers are also available; they come in a range of styles and prices.

Wire Whisks

Made of stainless steel wires that loop to form a bulbous shape, wire whisks are designed to aerate and mix. Larger balloon-type whisks are used for whipping air into ingredients such as egg whites and cream, while small and medium whisks are used for stirring hot mixtures as they cook and blending ingredients together without beating a lot of air into the mixture. When purchasing whisks, choose those that have sturdy wires and handles that are easy to grip. You can also find whisks that have their wires coated in heat-resistant silicone. These are a great choice if you prefer nonstick cookware, as the silicone coating prevents the wires from scratching the finish of your pots and pans. Avoid whisks with wires made of plastic, as they will not hold up well.

Piping

There are a million ways to frost a cupcake. Frosting can be spread on with a narrow spatula for a homey appearance or piped in any number of patterns if you are looking for more flair. You can use a large round tip to make soft swirls of frosting or a large star tip to give your cupcakes a sharper appearance. You can pipe frosting in one continuous line or pipe large dots all over the surface of the cupcake. It all depends on how much time and effort you want to put into collecting and mastering the many available decorating tips available. Following are some basic piping techniques that will be useful for the recipes in this book. For most cupcakes that are not designed to resemble something specific, like an animal or pattern, you can apply the frosting however you want. Feel free to get creative!

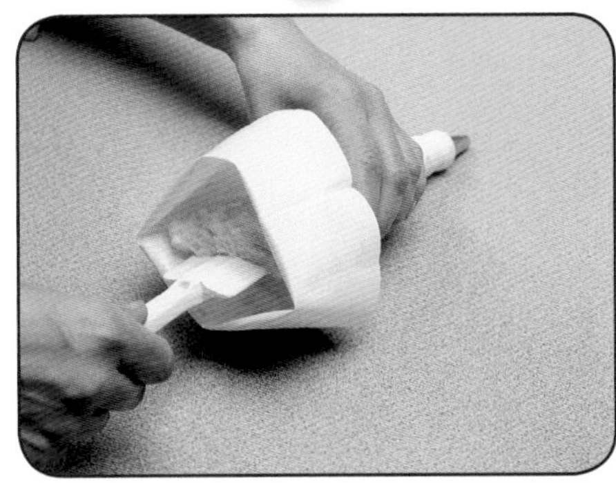

For each of the following piping techniques, you'll need a decorating bag fitted with the appropriate tip and filled with frosting. To fill a decorating bag, cut off a small piece of the bottom of the bag to create an opening, if necessary, and insert the decorating tip. Fold the top of the bag down and place the frosting in the bag. In general, fill the bag half to two-thirds full, then unfold the top of the bag. Do not fill the bag too full. (If you only need a small amount of frosting, use at least ¼ cup to get enough frosting for piping.) To prevent the frosting from squeezing out the top of the bag, twist the top tightly against the frosting. Place the twisted end of the bag in the palm of your writing hand with fingers positioned near the bag opening. Place your other hand under the bag to guide the tip.

When piping, hold the bag so the tip is at the angle indicated for the technique. Then, gently squeeze the bag from the top, using even pressure while guiding the tip with your other hand. Squeeze mainly with the palm of your hand rather than your fingers. Be careful not to loosen your grip on the twisted end or the frosting

will begin to push up and out of the top of the bag. The size of the decorations you pipe depends on how hard you squeeze as well as on the size of the opening in the tip.

Line (use a writing or small star tip): Hold the bag so the tip is at a 45-degree angle to the right. While gently squeezing the bag, guide the tip opening just above the cupcake in a curved, zigzag, squiggly or straight line. To end the line, stop squeezing, then lift the tip straight up.

Writing (use a writing tip): Hold the bag so the tip is at a 45-degree angle to the right for horizontal lines and toward you for vertical lines. While gently squeezing the bag, guide the tip opening just above the cupcake to form print or script letters. Stop squeezing, then lift the tip at the end of each letter for print letters and at the end of each word for script writing.

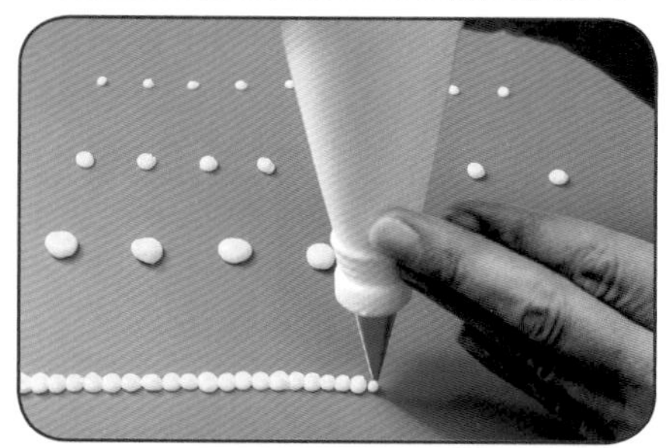

Dot (use a round tip): Hold the bag so the tip is at a 90-degree angle. Position the opening just above the cupcake and gently squeeze. Lift slightly while still squeezing. When the dot is of the desired size, stop squeezing, then lift the tip straight up.

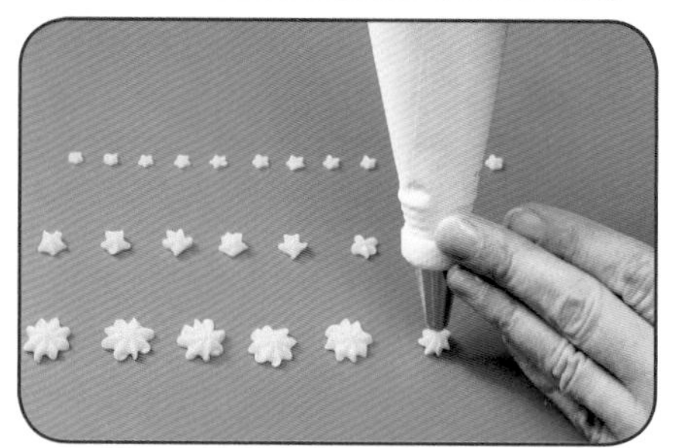

Star (use a star tip): Hold the bag so the tip is at a 90-degree angle. Position the opening just above the cupcake and gently squeeze. Lift slightly while still squeezing. When the star is of the desired size, stop squeezing, then lift the tip straight up.

Baker's Substitutions

Using the exact ingredients listed in a recipe helps produce the most consistent results, but sometimes that just isn't possible. If you can't find a particular ingredient or you run out of something at the last minute, you can often make a substitution without changing the finished product too much. The following suggested exchanges may allow you to finish your recipe; however, you should not make more than one substitution per recipe in order to ensure the best chances of delicious success.

If you don't have:	*Use:*
1 cup packed brown sugar	1 cup granulated sugar mixed with 2 tablespoons molasses
1 cup powdered sugar	1 cup granulated sugar plus 1 tablespoon cornstarch, processed in blender or food processor until powdery
1 teaspoon baking powder	¼ teaspoon baking soda plus ½ teaspoon cream of tartar
1 cup whole milk	1 cup skim milk plus 2 tablespoons melted butter
1 cup buttermilk	1 tablespoon lemon juice or vinegar plus milk to equal 1 cup (Stir; let mixture stand 5 minutes.)
1 cup sour cream	1 cup plain yogurt
1 cup molasses	1 cup dark corn syrup or honey
½ cup corn syrup	½ cup granulated sugar plus 2 tablespoons liquid
½ cup raisins	½ cup currants, dried cranberries, chopped dates or chopped prunes
1 ounce (1 square) unsweetened chocolate	3 tablespoons unsweetened cocoa powder plus 1 tablespoon shortening
1 ounce (1 square) semisweet baking chocolate	1 ounce unsweetened chocolate plus 1 tablespoon sugar
1 cup semisweet chocolate chips	6 ounces semisweet baking chocolate, chopped
1 teaspoon grated lemon or orange peel	½ teaspoon dried lemon or orange peel
1 teaspoon pumpkin pie spice	½ teaspoon ground cinnamon, ¼ teaspoon ground ginger, ⅛ teaspoon ground allspice and ⅛ teaspoon ground nutmeg

Spring Celebrations

Easter Chicks

- 1 package (about 18 ounces) yellow cake mix, plus ingredients to prepare mix
- 2 containers (16 ounces each) white frosting
- Pink and yellow food coloring
- Orange chewy fruit candy squares
- Black decorating gel

1. Preheat oven to 350°F. Line 60 mini (1¾-inch) muffin cups with paper baking cups. Prepare cake mix according to package directions. Spoon batter into prepared muffin cups, filling half full.

2. Bake 10 minutes or until toothpick inserted into centers comes out clean. Cool in pans 5 minutes. Remove to wire racks; cool completely. Use serrated knife to cut off rounded domes of cupcakes so that tops are flat.

3. Divide frosting between two small bowls; add food coloring, a few drops at a time, until desired shades are reached.

4. Remove baking cups from half of cupcakes. Spread small amount of frosting in center of cupcakes with baking cups. Set remaining cupcakes (without baking cups) upside down over frosting; press gently to seal cupcakes together. Frost cupcakes in desired colors, mounding extra frosting on top to create egg shape.

5. Working with one at a time, unwrap candy squares and microwave on LOW (30%) 5 to 10 seconds or until softened. Press candies between hands or on waxed paper to flatten to ⅛-inch thickness. Use scissors or paring knife to cut out triangles for beaks. Create faces on chicks with candy beaks and black decorating gel for eyes. *Makes 30 chicks*

Key Lime Pie Cupcakes

1 package (about 18 ounces) lemon cake mix with pudding in the mix
1 cup vegetable oil
4 eggs
¾ cup key lime juice,* divided
½ cup water
1 teaspoon grated lime peel
2 cups whipping cream
½ cup powdered sugar
Lime wedges or additional grated lime peel (optional)

**If you cannot find key lime juice, substitute regular lime juice.*

1. Preheat oven to 350°F. Line 24 standard (2½-inch) muffin cups with paper baking cups.

2. Combine cake mix, oil, eggs, ½ cup key lime juice, water and lime peel in large bowl; whisk 2 minutes or until thick and smooth. Spoon batter into prepared muffin cups, filling two-thirds full. Bake 20 minutes or until toothpick inserted into centers comes out clean. Cool in pans 10 minutes. Remove to wire racks; cool completely.

3. Beat cream in medium bowl with electric mixer at medium speed 3 to 5 minutes or until soft peaks form. Add sugar and remaining ¼ cup key lime juice; beat at medium-high speed 30 seconds or until medium-stiff peaks form.

4. Top each cupcake with dollop of whipped cream. Garnish with lime wedges.

Makes 24 cupcakes

Lazy Daisy Cupcakes

1 package (about 18 ounces) yellow cake mix, plus ingredients to prepare mix
Yellow food coloring
1 container (16 ounces) vanilla frosting
30 large marshmallows
24 small round candies or gumdrops

1. Preheat oven to 350°F. Line 24 standard (2½-inch) muffin cups with paper baking cups or spray with nonstick cooking spray.

2. Prepare cake mix according to package directions. Spoon batter into prepared muffin cups, filling two-thirds full. Bake 20 minutes or until toothpick inserted into centers comes out clean. Cool in pans 10 minutes. Remove to wire racks; cool completely.

3. Add food coloring to frosting in small bowl, a few drops at a time, until desired shade of yellow is reached. Frost cupcakes.

4. Cut each marshmallow crosswise into 4 pieces with scissors. Stretch pieces into petal shapes; place 5 pieces on each cupcake to form flower. Place round candy in center of each flower.

Makes 24 cupcakes

Key Lime Pie Cupcakes

Chocolate Easter Baskets

- 1 package (about 18 ounces) chocolate cake mix, plus ingredients to prepare mix
- 22 (3-inch) chewy chocolate candies
- Colored candy dots or decors (optional)
- 1 container (16 ounces) chocolate frosting
- Edible Easter grass (see Note)
- Candy-coated chocolate eggs, gumdrops or jelly beans

1. Preheat oven to 350°F. Line 24 standard (2½-inch) muffin cups with paper baking cups. Prepare cake mix according to package directions. Spoon batter into prepared muffin cups, filling two-thirds full.

2. Bake 20 minutes or until toothpick inserted into centers comes out clean. Cool in pans 10 minutes. Remove to wire racks; cool completely.

3. For each basket handle, unwrap one chocolate candy and microwave on LOW (30%) 6 to 8 seconds to soften. Stretch or roll candy between hands until about 6 inches long. Bend candy into handle shape; pinch ends slightly to make them pointed. If desired, attach candy dots to handles with very small amount of frosting. Place handles on waxed paper until set.

4. Frost cupcakes. Arrange basket handles on cupcakes. Place small mound of grass in center of each cupcake; top with chocolate eggs or other candies. *Makes 24 cupcakes*

Note: Edible Easter grass can be found seasonally at some candy and specialty stores. If it is not available, substitute tinted coconut. To tint coconut, dilute a few drops of green food coloring with ½ teaspoon water in a large food storage bag. Add 1 to 1½ cups flaked coconut; seal the bag and shake well until the coconut is evenly coated. For a deeper color, add additional diluted food coloring and shake again.

Strawberry Milkshake Cupcakes

- 2 cups all-purpose flour
- 1½ cups granulated sugar
- 4 teaspoons baking powder
- ½ teaspoon salt
- 1¼ cups (2½ sticks) unsalted butter, softened, divided
- 1 cup plus 6 to 8 tablespoons milk, divided
- 2 teaspoons vanilla, divided
- 3 eggs
- 2 containers (7 ounces each) plain Greek yogurt
- 1 cup seedless strawberry preserves
- 6 cups powdered sugar, divided
- ¼ cup shortening
- Pink gel food coloring
- Assorted decors

1. Preheat oven to 350°F. Line 24 standard (2½-inch) muffin cups with paper baking cups.

2. Beat flour, granulated sugar, baking powder and salt in large bowl with electric mixer at low speed until blended. Add ½ cup butter; beat at medium speed 30 seconds. Add 1 cup milk and 1 teaspoon vanilla; beat 2 minutes. Add eggs; beat 2 minutes. Spoon batter evenly into prepared baking cups.

3. Bake 20 minutes or until toothpick inserted into centers comes out clean. Cool in pans 10 minutes. Remove to wire racks; cool completely.

4. For filling, combine yogurt and preserves in medium bowl. Transfer to piping bag fitted with medium round tip. Press tip into top of each cupcake and squeeze bag to fill.

5. For frosting, beat 3 cups powdered sugar, remaining ¾ cup butter, shortening, 4 tablespoons milk and remaining 1 teaspoon vanilla in large bowl with electric mixer at low speed until smooth. Add remaining 3 cups powdered sugar and food coloring; beat until light and fluffy, adding remaining milk, 1 tablespoon at a time, as needed for desired consistency.

6. Pipe or spread frosting onto cupcakes. Decorate as desired.

Makes 24 cupcakes

Leprechaun Cupcakes

- 1 package (about 18 ounces) yellow or white cake mix, plus ingredients to prepare mix
- 1 container (16 ounces) vanilla frosting
- Chocolate wafer cookies
- Green food coloring
- Yellow chewy fruit candy squares
- Black licorice ropes and strings
- Black decorating gel
- White decors
- Red gumdrops
- Orange decorating icing

1. Preheat oven to 350°F. Line 24 standard (2½-inch) muffin cups with paper baking cups. Prepare cake mix according to package directions. Spoon batter into prepared muffin cups, filling two-thirds full.

2. Bake 20 minutes or until toothpick inserted into centers comes out clean. Cool in pans 10 minutes. Remove to wire racks; cool completely.

3. Trim chocolate wafer cookies into trapezoid shapes for hats. Place ½ cup frosting in small bowl. Add food coloring, a few drops at a time, until desired shade of green is reached. Spread green frosting over wafer cookies. Frost cupcakes with remaining white frosting.

4. Working with one at a time, unwrap chewy candy squares and microwave on LOW (30%) 5 seconds or until slightly softened. Press candy between hands or on waxed paper to flatten slightly; trim into square shapes for hat buckles. Trim licorice ropes into 2- to 3-inch lengths for hat brims. Press frosted wafers onto one edge of cupcakes. Adhere brims and buckles using dots of black decorating gel.

5. Roll out red gumdrops on generously sugared surface. Cut out small pieces to resemble mouths; place on cupcakes. Place decors on cupcakes for eyes; pipe dot of gel in center of each decor. Trim licorice strings and place on cupcakes for eyebrows. Pipe orange decorating icing around edges of cupcakes for beards and sideburns.

Makes 24 cupcakes

Marshmallow Delights

- 2 cups all-purpose flour
- 1 teaspoon baking soda
- 1 teaspoon baking powder
- ½ teaspoon salt
- ½ cup sour cream
- ½ cup milk
- 1 teaspoon vanilla
- 1 cup granulated sugar
- ½ cup (1 stick) butter, softened
- 2 eggs
- 1½ cups prepared white frosting
- Green food coloring
- 3 cups fruit-flavored mini marshmallows
- Green decorating sugar (optional)

1. Preheat oven to 350°F. Line 12 standard (2½-inch) muffin cups with paper baking cups. Sift flour, baking soda, baking powder and salt into medium bowl. Combine sour cream, milk and vanilla in small bowl.

2. Beat granulated sugar and butter in large bowl with electric mixer at medium speed 2 minutes or until fluffy. Add eggs, one at a time, beating well after each addition. Add flour mixture alternately with sour cream mixture, beginning and ending with flour mixture, beating well after each addition. Spoon batter evenly into prepared muffin cups.

3. Bake 20 minutes or until toothpick inserted into centers comes out clean. Cool in pan 10 minutes. Remove to wire rack; cool completely.

4. Place frosting in small bowl. Add food coloring, a few drops at a time, until desired shade of green is reached. Frost cupcakes. Arrange marshmallows over frosting; sprinkle with decorating sugar, if desired.

Makes 12 cupcakes

Lemon-Cream Cheese Cupcakes

- 1 package (2-layer size) white cake mix
- 1 package (4-serving size) JELL-O® Lemon Flavor Instant Pudding & Pie Filling
- 1 cup water
- 4 egg whites
- 2 tablespoons oil
- 1 package (16 ounces) powdered sugar
- 1 package (8 ounces) PHILADELPHIA® Cream Cheese, softened
- ¼ cup (½ stick) butter, softened
- 2 tablespoons lemon juice

PREHEAT oven to 350°F. Beat cake mix, dry pudding mix, water, egg whites and oil in large bowl with electric mixer on low speed until moistened. (Batter will be thick.) Beat on medium speed 2 minutes. Spoon batter evenly into 24 paper-lined 2½-inch muffin cups.

BAKE 21 to 24 minutes or until wooden toothpick inserted in centers comes out clean. Cool in pans 10 minutes; remove to wire racks. Cool completely.

BEAT sugar, cream cheese, butter and juice with electric mixer on low speed until well blended. Frost cupcakes.

Makes 24 cupcakes

Jazz It Up: Stir 1 teaspoon grated lemon peel into frosting mixture.

Prep Time: 10 minutes
Bake Time: 21 to 24 minutes

Friendly Frogs

- 1 package (about 18 ounces) cake mix, any flavor, plus ingredients to prepare mix
- 1 container (16 ounces) white frosting
- Green food coloring
- Green decorating sugar (optional)
- Black round candies or candy-coated chocolate pieces
- White chocolate candy discs
- Black and red string licorice
- Green jelly candy fruit slices

1. Preheat oven to 350°F. Line 24 standard (2½-inch) muffin cups with paper baking cups. Prepare cake mix according to package directions. Spoon batter into prepared muffin cups, filling two-thirds full.

2. Bake 20 minutes or until toothpick inserted into centers comes out clean. Cool in pans 10 minutes. Remove to wire racks; cool completely.

3. Place frosting in small bowl. Add food coloring, a few drops at a time, until desired shade of green is reached. Frost cupcakes; sprinkle with decorating sugar, if desired.

4. Use small dab of frosting to attach black candies to white discs for eyes. Cut licorice into smaller lengths for mouths and noses. Arrange candies on cupcakes to create frog faces.

5. Use scissors to cut jelly candies into feet, if desired. Set cupcakes on candy feet when ready to serve.

Makes 24 cupcakes

Individual Flower Pot Cakes

18 (2½×4-inch) sterilized unglazed terra cotta pots (see Tip)

1 package (about 18 ounces) dark chocolate cake mix, plus ingredients to prepare mix

1 package (12 ounces) semisweet chocolate chips

8 to 10 chocolate sandwich cookies, broken

1 container (16 ounces) chocolate frosting

Green drinking straws

Lollipops, decorating icing and assorted candies

Spearmint leaves and gummy worms

1. Preheat oven to 350°F. Generously grease flower pots; line bottoms with greased parchment paper. Place pots in standard (2½-inch) muffin cups.

2. Prepare cake mix according to package directions; stir in chocolate chips. Spoon batter into pots, filling half full.

3. Bake 35 minutes or until toothpick inserted into centers comes out clean. Remove pots to wire racks; cool completely.

4. Place cookies in food processor; process using on/off pulsing action until coarse crumbs form.

5. Frost cakes with chocolate frosting. Sprinkle cookie crumbs over frosting to resemble dirt.

6. Push straws into each flower pot for stems; trim straws to different heights with scissors. Insert lollipops into straw stems. Decorate lollipops with decorating icing and assorted candies. Arrange spearmint leaves and gummy worms around base of lollipop flowers.

Makes 18 cakes

Tip

Terra cotta pots can be found in garden centers and hardware stores. The pots used in this recipe should be new and never used for gardening. To sterilize the pots before preparing these cakes, wash them thoroughly and allow to dry completely. Bake in a preheated 350°F oven for 3 hours. Remove to wire racks; cool completely.

Funny Bunnies

1 cup all-purpose flour
1 teaspoon baking powder
1 teaspoon ground cinnamon
½ teaspoon salt
¼ teaspoon baking soda
Pinch ground nutmeg
1 cup sugar
2 eggs, beaten
½ cup canola or vegetable oil
1 teaspoon vanilla
1½ cups grated carrots (about 3 medium)
12 standard marshmallows
1 container (16 ounces) cream cheese frosting, divided
Pink food coloring
Assorted pink and blue candies and decors
24 mini marshmallows
12 red chewy fruit candy squares

1. Preheat oven to 350°F. Line 12 standard (2½-inch) muffin cups with paper baking cups.

2. Whisk flour, baking powder, cinnamon, salt, baking soda and nutmeg in large bowl. Beat sugar, eggs, oil and vanilla in medium bowl until well blended. Add to flour mixture; mix well. Stir in carrots. Spoon batter evenly into prepared muffin cups.

3. Bake 24 minutes or until toothpick inserted into centers comes out clean. Cool in pans 10 minutes. Remove to wire racks; cool completely. Meanwhile, cut each standard marshmallow in half with scissors; stretch marshmallow slices slightly into oblong shape to create ears.

4. Reserve ½ cup frosting in small bowl. Frost cupcakes with remaining frosting. Add food coloring to reserved frosting, a few drops at a time, until desired shade of pink is reached. Pipe or spread pink frosting down center of each marshmallow slice. Arrange marshmallow ears on each cupcake.

5. Arrange pink and blue candies on cupcakes to create bunny faces. Press mini marshmallows to flatten slightly; add to bunny faces for cheeks. Working with one at a time, unwrap candy squares and microwave on LOW (30%) 5 seconds or just until softened. Pinch center of each candy half to form bow tie; place on cupcake.

Makes 12 cupcakes

Variation: To save time, use one package (about 18 ounces) carrot cake mix instead of preparing the cupcakes from scratch. A standard cake mix will make 22 to 24 cupcakes; decorate as many bunnies as desired and reserve the remaining cupcakes for another use.

Magically Minty Mini Cupcakes

- 1 package (about 18 ounces) chocolate cake mix, plus ingredients to prepare mix
- 2 teaspoons mint extract
- 1 container (16 ounces) white frosting
- Green and white sprinkles, green decorating sugar or shamrock candy decorations

1. Preheat oven to 350°F. Line 60 mini (1¾-inch) muffin cups with paper baking cups.
2. Prepare cake mix according to package directions; stir in mint extract. Spoon batter into prepared muffin cups, filling half full.
3. Bake 10 minutes or until toothpick inserted into centers comes out clean. Cool in pans 5 minutes. Remove to wire racks; cool completely. Frost cupcakes; decorate with sprinkles, sugar or candy decorations. *Makes 60 mini cupcakes*

Creamy Strawberry Cookie "Tarts"

- ⅔ cup boiling water
- 1 package (4-serving size) JELL-O® Brand Strawberry Flavor Gelatin
- 1 package (8 ounces) PHILADELPHIA® Cream Cheese, cubed
- 1 cup thawed COOL WHIP® Whipped Topping
- 12 CHIPS AHOY!® Real Chocolate Chip Cookies
- 12 small strawberries

STIR boiling water into dry gelatin mix in small bowl at least 2 minutes until completely dissolved. Cool 5 minutes, stirring occasionally.

POUR gelatin mixture into blender Add cream cheese; cover. Blend on medium speed 30 to 45 seconds or until well blended; scrape down side of blender container, if needed. Add whipped topping; cover. Blend on low speed 5 seconds or just until blended.

LINE 12 muffin pan cups with paper liners; spray with cooking spray. Place 1 cookie on bottom of each prepared cup; top evenly with the gelatin mixture. Refrigerate 1 hour 30 minutes or until firm. Top each with a strawberry just before serving. Store leftover desserts in refrigerator. *Makes 12 servings*

Prep Time: 15 minutes plus refrigerating

Magically Minty Mini Cupcakes

Lemon Meringue Cupcakes

- 1 package (about 18 ounces) lemon cake mix, plus ingredients to prepare mix
- ¾ cup prepared lemon curd*
- 4 egg whites, at room temperature
- 6 tablespoons sugar

**Lemon curd, a thick sweet lemon spread, is available in many supermarkets near the jams and preserves.*

1. Preheat oven to 350°F. Line 9 jumbo (3½-inch) muffin cups with paper baking cups. Prepare cake mix according to package directions. Spoon batter into prepared muffin cups, filling two-thirds full.

2. Bake 23 to 25 minutes or until toothpick inserted into centers comes out clean. Cool in pans 10 minutes. Remove to wire racks; cool completely. *Increase oven temperature to 375°F.*

3. Cut off tops of cupcakes with serrated knife. (Do not remove paper baking cups.) Scoop out small hole in center of each cupcake with tablespoon; fill with generous tablespoon lemon curd. Replace cupcake tops.

4. Beat egg whites in medium bowl with electric mixer at high speed until soft peaks form. Continue beating while gradually adding sugar; beat until stiff peaks form. Pipe or spread meringue in peaks on each cupcake.

5. Place cupcakes on baking sheet. Bake 5 minutes or until peaks of meringue are golden. *Makes 9 jumbo cupcakes*

Variation: This recipe can also be used to make 24 standard (2½-inch) cupcakes. Line muffin pans with paper baking cups; prepare and bake cake mix according to package directions. Cut off tops of cupcakes; scoop out hole in each cupcake with teaspoon and fill with generous teaspoon lemon curd. Pipe or spread about ⅓ cup meringue in peaks on each cupcake; bake as directed above.

Little Lamb Cakes

1 package (about 18 ounces) yellow cake mix, plus ingredients to prepare mix
1 container (16 ounces) vanilla frosting
15 large marshmallows
Pink jelly beans or decors
1 package (10½ ounces) mini marshmallows
Black string licorice
44 mini chocolate chips

1. Preheat oven to 350°F. Line 24 standard (2½-inch) muffin cups with paper baking cups. Prepare cake mix according to package directions. Spoon batter into prepared muffin cups, filling two-thirds full.

2. Bake 20 minutes or until toothpick inserted into centers comes out clean. Cool in pans 10 minutes. Remove to wire racks; cool completely.

3. Frost cupcakes. Cut each large marshmallow crosswise into 3 pieces. Stretch pieces into oval shapes; arrange on cupcakes to resemble ears. Attach pink jelly bean to each ear with frosting.

4. Press mini marshmallows into frosting around edge of cupcakes. Cut jelly beans in half crosswise; cut licorice into ½-inch pieces. Create faces with mini chips for eyes, half jelly bean for noses and licorice for mouths. *Makes 24 cupcakes*

Raindrop Cupcakes

1 package (2-layer size) white cake mix
1 package (4-serving size) JELL-O® Brand Berry Blue Flavor Gelatin
1 cup boiling water
1 tub (8 ounces) COOL WHIP® Whipped Topping, thawed
Decorating gel
Colored sugar (optional)

HEAT oven to 350°F.

PREPARE cake mix as directed on package, using egg whites. Spoon batter into paper-lined muffin pan, filling each cup ½ full. Bake as directed on package. Cool cupcakes in pan 15 minutes, then pierce with large fork at ¼-inch intervals.

DISSOLVE gelatin completely in boiling water in small bowl. Gradually spoon over cupcakes.

REFRIGERATE 3 to 4 hours. Frost with whipped topping. Draw umbrellas on cupcakes with decorating gel. Sprinkle with colored sugar. Store cupcakes in refrigerator. *Makes 24 cupcakes*

Little Lamb Cakes

Mini Bees

- 1 package (about 18 ounces) chocolate cake mix, plus ingredients to prepare mix
- 1 container (16 ounces) chocolate frosting
- 1½ cups prepared white frosting
- Yellow food coloring
- Black string licorice
- Yellow candy wafers

1. Preheat oven to 350°F. Line 60 mini (1¾-inch) muffin cups with paper baking cups. Prepare cake mix according to package directions. Spoon batter into prepared muffin cups, filling half full.

2. Bake 10 minutes or until toothpick inserted into centers comes out clean. Cool in pans 5 minutes. Remove to wire racks; cool completely.

3. Microwave chocolate frosting in medium microwavable bowl on LOW (30%) 30 seconds; stir until melted. Dip tops of cupcakes in melted frosting; place on baking sheet. (Frosting may need to be reheated several times to maintain melted consistency.) Refrigerate cupcakes 10 minutes or until frosting is set before adding stripes. Reserve remaining chocolate frosting.

4. Place white frosting in medium bowl; add food coloring, a few drops at a time, until desired shade of yellow is reached. Spoon frosting into pastry bag or resealable food storage bag with ⅛-inch corner cut off. Pipe stripes on cupcakes.

5. Pipe reserved chocolate frosting for eyes and mouths, reheating, if necessary, to achieve smooth consistency. Cut licorice into 1½-inch lengths; place on cupcakes just above eyes to resemble antennae and at opposite end to resemble tails. Cut candy wafers in half; arrange two halves on each cupcake to resemble wings.

Makes 60 bees

Easy Easter Cupcakes

1 package (about 18 ounces) yellow cake mix, plus ingredients to prepare mix
1 container (16 ounces) vanilla frosting
Green food coloring
24 sugar-coated colored marshmallow chicks and/or rabbits
Round white candies

1. Preheat oven to 350°F. Line 24 standard (2½-inch) muffin cups with paper baking cups. Prepare cake mix according to package directions. Spoon batter into prepared muffin cups, filling two-thirds full. Bake 20 minutes or until toothpick inserted into centers comes out clean. Cool in pans 10 minutes. Remove to wire racks; cool completely.

2. Tint frosting in small bowl, adding food coloring a few drops at a time until desired shade of green is reached. Frost cupcakes. Trim marshmallow animals with scissors or knife to fit on cupcakes. Place one marshmallow on each cupcake. Decorate edges of cupcakes with white candies.

Makes 24 cupcakes

Red's Rockin' Rainbow Cupcakes

2¼ cups all-purpose flour
1 tablespoon baking powder
½ teaspoon salt
1⅔ cups granulated sugar
½ cup (1 stick) butter, softened
1 cup milk
2 teaspoons vanilla extract
3 large egg whites
Blue and assorted food colorings
1½ cups "M&M's"® Chocolate Mini Baking Bits, divided
1 container (16 ounces) white frosting

Preheat oven to 350°F. Lightly grease 24 (2¾-inch) muffin cups or line with paper or foil liners; set aside. In large bowl combine flour, baking powder and salt. Blend in sugar, butter, milk and vanilla; beat about 2 minutes. Add egg whites; beat 2 minutes.

Divide batter evenly among prepared muffin cups. Place 2 drops desired food coloring into each muffin cup. Swirl gently with knife. Sprinkle evenly with ¾ cup "M&M's"® Chocolate Mini Baking Bits.

Bake 20 to 25 minutes or until toothpick inserted in center comes out clean. Cool completely on wire racks. Combine frosting and blue food coloring. Spread frosting over cupcakes; decorate with remaining ¾ cup "M&M's"® Chocolate Mini Baking Bits to make rainbows. Store in tightly covered container.

Makes 24 cupcakes

Easy Easter Cupcakes

Summer Sunshine

Dragonflies

1 package (about 18 ounces) cake mix, any flavor, plus ingredients to prepare mix
Almond bark or white chocolate candy discs
Pink, purple, yellow and green food coloring
44 small pretzel twists
22 pretzel sticks (about 3 inches)
1 container (16 ounces) white frosting
White and purple nonpareils
Silver dragees

1. Preheat oven to 350°F. Line 22 standard (2½-inch) muffin cups with paper baking cups. Prepare cake mix according to package directions. Spoon batter into prepared muffin cups, filling two-thirds full.

2. Bake 20 minutes or until toothpick inserted into centers comes out clean. Cool in pans 10 minutes. Remove to wire racks; cool completely.

3. Line large baking sheet with waxed paper. Melt almond bark according to package directions. Stir in pink food coloring, a few drops at a time, until desired shade of pink is reached. Dip pretzel twists in melted candy to coat; arrange two twists together on prepared baking sheet. Dip pretzel sticks in melted candy; place one stick between two pretzel twists to create dragonfly. Sprinkle pretzel twists with white nonpareils; arrange two purple nonpareils at top of pretzel sticks for eyes. Press dragees into bottom half of pretzel sticks. Let stand 10 minutes or until set.

4. Meanwhile, divide frosting between three small bowls. Add different food coloring (except pink) to each bowl, a few drops at a time, until desired colors are reached. Pipe or spread frosting on cupcakes; top with dragonflies.

Makes 22 cupcakes

Mini Fireworks

1 package (about 18 ounces) chocolate cake mix, plus ingredients to prepare mix
Prepared chocolate frosting
4 ounces almond bark or white chocolate candy discs
Red, white and blue decorating sugar

1. Preheat oven to 350°F. Line 60 mini (1¾-inch) muffin cups with paper baking cups. Prepare cake mix according to package directions. Spoon batter into prepared muffin cups, filling almost full.

2. Bake 10 minutes or until toothpick inserted into centers comes out clean. Cool in pans 5 minutes. Remove to wire racks; cool completely. Frost cupcakes.

3. Place large piece of waxed paper on work surface. Melt almond bark according to package directions; place in plastic squeeze bottle or piping bag fitted with small writing tip. Pipe firework shapes onto waxed paper, a few at a time. Sprinkle with colored sugar. Repeat to create 60 large or 120 small fireworks. Let stand 15 minutes. Stick fireworks into frosting.

Makes 60 mini cupcakes

Cherry Cupcakes

1 package (about 18 ounces) chocolate cake mix
3 eggs
1⅓ cups water
½ cup vegetable oil
1 (21-ounce) can cherry pie filling
1 container (16 ounces) vanilla frosting

Prepare cake mix according to package directions, using eggs, water and oil. Spoon batter into 24 paper-lined muffin pan cups, filling two-thirds full.

Remove 24 cherries from cherry filling; set aside. Spoon generous teaspoon of remaining cherry filling onto center of each cupcake.

Bake in preheated 350°F oven 20 to 25 minutes. Cool in pans on wire racks 10 minutes. Remove from pans. Let cool completely. Frost cupcakes with vanilla frosting. Garnish cupcakes with reserved cherries.

Makes 24 cupcakes

Favorite recipe from *Cherry Marketing Institute*

Mini Fireworks

Pink Lemonade Cupcakes

- 1 package (about 18 ounces) white cake mix *without* pudding in the mix
- 1 cup water
- 3 egg whites
- ⅓ cup plus ¼ cup frozen pink lemonade concentrate, divided
- 2 tablespoons vegetable oil
- 5 to 8 drops red food coloring, divided
- 4 cups powdered sugar
- ⅓ cup butter, softened
- Lemon slice candies (optional)

1. Preheat oven to 350°F. Line 24 standard (2½-inch) muffin cups with paper baking cups.
2. Beat cake mix, water, egg whites, ⅓ cup lemonade concentrate, oil and 4 to 6 drops food coloring in large bowl with electric mixer at medium speed 2 minutes or until well blended. Spoon batter evenly into prepared muffin cups.
3. Bake 20 minutes or until toothpick inserted into centers comes out clean. Cool in pans 10 minutes. Remove to wire racks; cool completely.
4. Beat powdered sugar, butter and remaining ¼ cup lemonade concentrate in medium bowl with electric mixer at medium speed until well blended. Beat in remaining 1 to 2 drops food coloring until desired shade of pink is reached.
5. Spread frosting over cupcakes. Garnish with candies.

Makes 24 cupcakes

Tip: To make these colorful cupcakes look even more like glasses of refreshing pink lemonade, you can trim bendable plastic straws to fit and press them into the top of cupcakes.

Colorful Caterpillar Cupcakes

- 1 package (about 18 ounces) vanilla cake mix
- 1¼ cups water
- 3 eggs
- ⅓ cup vegetable oil
- Assorted food coloring
- 1 cup (2 sticks) unsalted butter, softened
- 1 teaspoon vanilla
- 1 teaspoon orange extract
- ¼ teaspoon salt
- 1 tablespoon meringue powder
- 1 tablespoon milk
- 1 package (16 ounces) powdered sugar
- Assorted candies, candy-coated chocolate pieces, red string licorice and lollipops
- Gummy worms

1. Preheat oven to 350°F. Line 20 standard (2½-inch) muffin cups with paper baking cups.*

2. Beat cake mix, water, eggs and oil in large bowl with electric mixer at low speed 30 seconds. Beat at medium speed 2 minutes or until well blended. Divide batter between five bowls; tint each bowl with different color food coloring. Spoon batter into prepared muffin cups, filling three-fourths full.

3. Bake 20 minutes or until toothpick inserted into centers comes out clean. Cool in pans 10 minutes. Remove to wire racks; cool completely.

4. Beat butter, vanilla, orange extract and salt in medium bowl with electric mixer at medium-high speed until fluffy. Beat in meringue powder and milk. Gradually add powdered sugar until well blended. Beat at high speed 5 minutes or until frosting is light and fluffy.

5. Set aside two cupcakes for caterpillar head. Frost remaining cupcakes. Place one cupcake on its side towards one end of serving platter. Place second cupcake on its side next to first cupcake; arrange remaining cupcakes, alternating colors, in row to create body of caterpillar.

6. Frost one reserved cupcake; decorate with assorted candies, chocolate pieces, licorice and lollipops to create face. Place plain cupcake upright at front of cupcake row for head; top with face cupcake on its side. Cut gummy worms into small pieces; attach to caterpillar body with frosting to create legs.

Makes 20 cupcakes

**Use white paper baking cups to best show colors of caterpillar.*

Patriotic Cocoa Cupcakes

- 2 cups sugar
- 1¾ cups all-purpose flour
- ¾ cup HERSHEY'S® Cocoa
- 2 teaspoons baking soda
- 1 teaspoon baking powder
- 1 teaspoon salt
- 2 eggs
- 1 cup buttermilk or sour milk*
- 1 cup boiling water
- ½ cup vegetable oil
- 1 teaspoon vanilla extract
- Vanilla Frosting (recipe follows)
- Chocolate stars or blue and red decorating icings (in tubes)

**To sour milk: Use 1 tablespoon white vinegar plus milk to equal 1 cup.*

1. Heat oven to 350°F. Grease and flour muffin cups (2½ inches in diameter) or line with paper bake cups.

2. Combine dry ingredients in large bowl. Add eggs, buttermilk, water, oil and vanilla; beat on medium speed of mixer 2 minutes (batter will be thin). Fill cups ⅔ full with batter.

3. Bake 15 minutes or until wooden pick inserted in center comes out clean. Remove cupcakes from pan. Cool completely.

4. To make chocolate stars for garnish, if desired, cut several cupcakes into ½-inch slices; cut out star shapes from cake slices. Frost remaining cupcakes. Garnish with chocolate stars or with blue and red decorating icings.

Makes about 30 cupcakes

Vanilla Frosting: Beat ¼ cup (½ stick) softened butter, ¼ cup shortening and 2 teaspoons vanilla extract in large bowl. Add 1 cup powdered sugar; beat until creamy. Add 3 cups powdered sugar alternately with 3 to 4 tablespoons milk, beating to spreading consistency. Makes about 2⅓ cups.

Tangy Raspberry Minis

- 1 cup all-purpose flour
- ½ teaspoon baking powder
- ½ teaspoon baking soda
- ½ cup granulated sugar
- ¼ cup (½ stick) unsalted butter, softened
- 1 egg
- ½ teaspoon vanilla
- ½ cup buttermilk
- 24 fresh raspberries
- 2 tablespoons coarse sugar
- 2 cups powdered sugar
- 6 to 9 tablespoons milk, divided

1. Preheat oven to 350°F. Line 24 mini (1¾-inch) muffin cups with paper baking cups; spray with nonstick cooking spray.

2. Whisk flour, baking powder and baking soda in small bowl. Beat granulated sugar and butter in large bowl with electric mixer at medium speed until creamy. Add egg and vanilla; beat until blended. Add flour mixture and buttermilk; beat at low speed just until combined.

3. Spoon batter evenly into prepared muffin cups. Place 1 raspberry on top of batter in each cup. Sprinkle evenly with coarse sugar.

4. Bake 15 minutes or until light brown. Cool in pans 5 minutes. Remove to wire rack; cool completely.

5. Meanwhile, whisk powdered sugar and 6 tablespoons milk in medium bowl until smooth. Add remaining milk, 1 tablespoon at a time, to make pourable glaze. Drizzle over cupcakes.

Makes 24 mini cupcakes

Graduation Party Cupcakes

- 1 package (about 18 ounces) white cake mix
- 1¼ cups water
- ⅓ cup vegetable oil
- 3 egg whites
- Food coloring in school colors
- 1 container (16 ounces) white frosting
- 22 chocolate squares
- Gummy candy strips
- 22 mini candy-coated chocolate pieces

1. Preheat oven to 325°F. Line 22 standard (2½-inch) muffin cups with paper baking cups.

2. Beat cake mix, water, oil and egg whites in large bowl with electric mixer at medium speed 2 minutes or until blended. Tint batter with one food coloring, a few drops at a time, until desired shade is reached. Spoon batter into prepared muffin cups, filling two-thirds full.

3. Bake 20 minutes or until toothpick inserted into centers comes out clean. Cool in pans 10 minutes. Remove to wire racks; cool completely.

4. Tint frosting in small bowl with other food coloring, a few drops at a time, until desired shade is reached. Frost cupcakes.

5. Place chocolate square on top of each cupcake. Place small dab of frosting in center of squares; attach candy strips for tassel and chocolate piece for button. *Makes 22 cupcakes*

Ice Cream Cone Cupcakes

- 24 flat-bottomed ice cream cones
- 1 package (about 18 ounces) white cake mix, plus ingredients to prepare mix
- 2 tablespoons nonpareils
- Prepared vanilla and chocolate frostings
- Additional nonpareils and decors

1. Preheat oven to 350°F. Stand ice cream cones in 13×9-inch baking pan or muffin cups.

2. Prepare cake mix according to package directions; stir in nonpareils. Spoon batter evenly into cones.

3. Bake 20 minutes or until toothpick inserted into centers comes out clean. Remove to wire racks; cool completely.

4. Frost cupcakes and decorate as desired.

Makes 24 cupcakes

Note: These cupcakes are best served the day they are made.

Graduation Party Cupcakes

Hidden Berry Cupcakes

- 1¾ cups all-purpose flour
- 1¼ cups granulated sugar
- 1 tablespoon baking powder
- ½ teaspoon salt
- ⅓ cup (5 tablespoons plus 1 teaspoon) butter, softened
- 3 eggs
- ⅔ cup milk
- 1 tablespoon vanilla
- 1 cup QUAKER® Oats (quick or old fashioned, uncooked)
- ½ cup seedless strawberry or raspberry fruit spread
- Confectioners' sugar

1. Heat oven to 350°F. Line 16 medium muffin cups with paper or foil liners. Set aside.

2. Combine flour, sugar, baking powder and salt in large bowl. Add butter and beat with electric mixer on low speed until crumbly, about 1 minute. Combine eggs, milk and vanilla in medium bowl; add to flour mixture. Beat on low speed until incorporated, then on medium speed 2 minutes. Gently fold in oats. Divide batter evenly among muffin cups, filling each about ¾ full.

3. Bake 18 minutes or until a wooden pick inserted in center comes out clean. Remove from pan; cool completely on wire rack.

4. Using small sharp knife, cut cone-shaped piece from center of each cupcake, leaving ¾-inch border around edge of cupcake. Carefully remove and reserve cake pieces. Fill each depression with generous teaspoon of fruit spread. Top with reserved cake pieces; sift confectioners' sugar over tops of cupcakes.

Makes 16 cupcakes

Play Ball

- 2 cups plus 1 tablespoon all-purpose flour, divided
- ¾ cup granulated sugar
- ¾ cup packed brown sugar
- 1 tablespoon baking powder
- 1 teaspoon salt
- ½ teaspoon baking soda
- 1¼ cups milk
- 3 eggs
- ½ cup shortening
- 1½ teaspoons vanilla
- ½ cup mini semisweet chocolate chips
- 1 container (16 ounces) vanilla frosting
- Assorted candies and food colorings

1. Preheat oven to 350°F. Line 24 standard (2½-inch) muffin cups with paper baking cups.

2. Combine 2 cups flour, granulated sugar, brown sugar, baking powder, salt and baking soda in medium bowl. Beat milk, eggs, shortening and vanilla in large bowl with electric mixer at medium speed until well blended. Add flour mixture; beat at high speed 3 minutes, scraping side of bowl frequently.

3. Toss chocolate chips with remaining 1 tablespoon flour in small bowl; stir into batter. Spoon batter evenly into prepared muffin cups.

4. Bake 20 minutes or until toothpick inserted into centers comes out clean. Cool in pans 10 minutes. Remove to wire racks; cool completely. Decorate with frosting and candies to resemble baseballs, basketballs and/or soccer balls.

Makes 24 cupcakes

Tropical Luau Cupcakes

- 2 cans (8 ounces each) crushed pineapple in juice
- 1 package (about 18 ounces) yellow cake mix *without* pudding in the mix
- 1 package (4-serving size) banana cream instant pudding and pie filling mix
- 4 eggs
- 1⁄3 cup vegetable oil
- 1⁄4 teaspoon ground nutmeg
- 1 container (12 ounces) whipped vanilla frosting
- 3⁄4 cup shredded coconut, toasted*
- 3 to 4 medium kiwi
- 30 (2½-inch) pretzel sticks

**To toast coconut, spread evenly on ungreased baking sheet. Toast in preheated 350°F oven 5 to 7 minutes or until light golden brown, stirring occasionally.*

1. Preheat oven to 350°F. Line 30 standard (2½-inch) muffin cups with paper baking cups. Drain pineapple, reserving juice. Set pineapple aside.

2. Beat cake mix, pudding mix, eggs, oil, reserved pineapple juice and nutmeg in large bowl with electric mixer at low speed 1 minute or until blended. Beat at medium speed 2 minutes or until smooth. Fold in pineapple. Spoon batter into prepared muffin cups, filling two-thirds full.

3. Bake 20 minutes or until toothpick inserted into centers comes out clean. Cool in pans 10 minutes. Remove to wire racks; cool completely.

4. Frost cupcakes; sprinkle with coconut.

5. For palm trees,** peel kiwi and cut into 1⁄8-inch-thick slices. Cut small notches around edges of kiwi slices to resemble palm fronds. For palm tree trunk, push pretzel stick into, but not through, center of each kiwi slice. Push other end of pretzel into top of each cupcake.

Makes 30 cupcakes

***Palm tree decorations can be made up to 1 hour before serving.*

All-American Cupcakes

1 package (about 18 ounces) cake mix, any flavor, plus ingredients to prepare mix
1 container (16 ounces) white frosting
Blue candy stars or blue mini candy-coated chocolate pieces
Red string licorice

1. Preheat oven to 350°F. Line 24 standard (2½-inch) muffin cups with paper baking cups. Prepare cake mix according to package directions. Spoon batter into prepared muffin cups, filling two-thirds full.

2. Bake 20 minutes or until toothpick inserted into centers comes out clean. Cool in pans 10 minutes. Remove to wire racks; cool completely.

3. Frost cupcakes. Arrange candy stars in left corner of each cupcake. Arrange licorice in rows across remaining portion of each cupcake, cutting pieces to fit.

Makes 24 cupcakes

Firecracker Cupcakes

1½ cups BAKER'S® ANGEL FLAKE® Coconut, divided
4 drops each blue and red food coloring
24 yellow cupcakes
2 cups thawed COOL WHIP® Whipped Topping
24 red string licorice pieces (4 inches)

PLACE ½ cup of the coconut in each of two separate resealable plastic bags; set remaining ½ cup coconut aside. Add blue food coloring to coconut in one bag and red food coloring to coconut in second bag. Seal bags; shake until coconut is evenly tinted.

SPREAD tops of cupcakes with whipped topping. Sprinkle with red, white (uncolored) and blue coconut as desired; press coconut gently into whipped topping to secure.

INSERT licorice piece into top of each cupcake for the "firecracker's fuse." Store in refrigerator.

Makes 24 cupcakes

Jazz It Up: Divide whipped topping into thirds. Color one third with 4 drops red food coloring and second third with 4 drops blue food coloring. Leave remaining whipped topping white. Spread onto cupcakes and continue as directed.

Prep Time: 10 minutes
Chill Time: 10 minutes

Under the Sea

- 1 package (about 18 ounces) cake mix, any flavor, plus ingredients to prepare mix
- 2 containers (16 ounces each) white frosting
- Blue, green, yellow, red and purple food coloring
- White decorating sugar (optional)
- Black decorating gel
- Assorted color decors, nonpareils and candy fish

1. Preheat oven to 350°F. Line 20 standard (2½-inch) muffin cups or spray with nonstick cooking spray. Prepare cake mix according to package directions. Spoon batter into prepared muffin cups, filling three-fourths full.

2. Bake 20 minutes or until toothpick inserted into centers comes out clean. Cool in pans 10 minutes. Remove to wire racks; cool completely.

3. Spoon one container of frosting into small bowl; add blue and green food coloring, a few drops at a time, until desired shade of aqua is reached. Spoon into pastry bag with large star decorating tip. Pipe frosting in swirl pattern on cupcakes. Sprinkle with decorating sugar, if desired.

4. Divide remaining frosting between four bowls; add different food coloring (except blue) to each bowl, a few drops at a time, until desired shades are reached. Spoon each color into pastry bags with round decorating tip or food storage bags with small corner cut off. Pipe sea creatures and plants on cupcakes: yellow fish, red crabs, purple starfish and green seaweed. Decorate with decorating gel, decors and candies. *Makes 20 cupcakes*

Strawberry Preserve Cupcakes

- 1 package (about 18 ounces) moist strawberry cake mix
- 2 cups sour cream
- 3 eggs
- ¼ cup water
- ⅓ cup POLANER® All Fruit Strawberry Spreadable Fruit
- 24 paper baking cups

PREHEAT oven to 350°F. Line 2 muffin pans with paper baking cups.

COMBINE cake mix, sour cream, eggs and water in a large bowl. Stir with a spoon and/or whisk until well blended. Fill paper-lined muffin cups one-half full with batter. Using a spoon, make a slight indentation in the center of each cup; fill with a heaping ½ teaspoonful of strawberry spreadable fruit. Spoon remaining batter evenly over each filled cup; covering spreadable fruit. (Muffin cups should be about ¾ full).

BAKE 20 to 30 minutes or until a toothpick comes out clean. (If toothpick goes through spreadable fruit, it will not come out clean.) Cool for 1 minute and remove from pans. Cool completely before adding icing and toppings, as desired. Store in the refrigerator. *Makes 24 cupcakes*

Prep Time: 15 minutes
Start-to-Finish Time: 35 minutes

S'more-Topped Cupcakes

- 1¼ cups all-purpose flour
- ½ cup unsweetened cocoa powder
- ¾ teaspoon baking soda
- ½ teaspoon salt
- ½ cup (1 stick) butter, softened
- 1¼ cups sugar
- 2 eggs
- 1 cup milk
- 1 teaspoon vanilla
- 6 whole graham crackers (12 squares)
- 1½ cups marshmallow creme
- 1½ bars (3 to 4 ounces each) milk chocolate, chopped into ½-inch chunks

1. Preheat oven to 350°F. Line 12 standard (2½-inch) muffin cups with paper baking cups. Sift flour, cocoa, baking soda and salt into medium bowl.

2. Beat butter in large bowl with electric mixer at medium speed until creamy. Add sugar; beat 3 minutes. Add eggs, one at a time, beating well after each addition. Combine milk and vanilla in measuring cup. Add flour mixture and milk mixture alternately to batter, beginning and ending with flour mixture. Spoon batter into prepared muffin cups, filling three-fourths full.

3. Bake 20 minutes or until toothpick inserted into centers comes out clean. Cool in pan 10 minutes. Remove to wire rack; cool completely.

4. Break each graham cracker square into ¾-inch pieces; press onto each cupcake to completely cover top and extend slightly over edge of cupcake. Spread about 2 tablespoons marshmallow creme over each cupcake (see Note); top with chocolate chunks. Freeze cupcakes 15 minutes.

5. Preheat broiler. Place cupcakes on baking sheet. Broil 6 inches from heat 1 minute or until marshmallow creme is lightly browned. Serve immediately.

Makes 12 cupcakes

Note: Marshmallow creme is very sticky and can be difficult to spread. Spray your utensils with nonstick cooking spray; drop teaspoon-size dollops of marshmallow creme over graham crackers and spread gently to cover.

Margarita Cupcakes

- 1 package (about 18 ounces) white cake mix
- ¾ cup plus 2 tablespoons margarita mix, divided
- 2 eggs
- ⅓ cup vegetable oil
- ¼ cup water
- 3 teaspoons grated lime peel (about 3 limes), divided
- Juice of 1 lime
- 2 tablespoons tequila or lime juice
- 3 cups powdered sugar
- 1 tablespoon white decorating or granulated sugar
- 1 tablespoon salt (optional)
- Green and yellow food coloring
- Lime peel strips (optional)

1. Preheat oven to 350°F. Line 24 standard (2½-inch) muffin cups with paper baking cups.

2. Combine cake mix, ¾ cup margarita mix, eggs, oil, water, 1 teaspoon lime peel and lime juice in large bowl. Whisk 2 minutes or until well blended. Spoon batter evenly into prepared muffin cups.

3. Bake 20 minutes or until toothpick inserted into centers comes out clean. Cool in pans 10 minutes. Remove cupcakes to wire racks; cool completely.

4. Combine tequila, remaining 2 tablespoons margarita mix and 2 teaspoons lime peel in medium bowl. Gradually whisk in powdered sugar until desired glaze consistency is reached. Combine decorating sugar and salt, if desired, in small bowl. Add food coloring, one drop at a time, until desired shade of green is reached.

5. Spread glaze over cupcakes; dip edges in sugar-salt mixture. Garnish with lime peel strips.

Makes 24 cupcakes

Fall Flavors

Apple Cider Cupcakes

- 1 package (about 18 ounces) spice cake mix
- 1¼ cups apple cider
- ⅓ cup vegetable oil
- 3 eggs
- 2 cups coarsely chopped walnuts, plus additional for garnish
- Apple Cider Frosting (recipe follows)

1. Preheat oven to 350°F. Line 24 standard (2½-inch) muffin cups with paper baking cups.

2. Beat cake mix, apple cider, oil and eggs in medium bowl with electric mixer at low speed until blended; beat at medium speed 2 minutes. Stir in 2 cups chopped walnuts. Spoon batter evenly into prepared muffin cups.

3. Bake 20 minutes or until toothpick inserted into centers comes out clean. Cool in pans 10 minutes. Remove to wire racks; cool completely.

4. Prepare Apple Cider Frosting; frost cupcakes. Garnish with additional chopped walnuts. *Makes 24 cupcakes*

Apple Cider Frosting: Beat ½ cup (1 stick) softened unsalted butter and ¼ cup apple cider in medium bowl with electric mixer at low speed until well blended. Gradually beat in 4 cups powdered sugar until smooth. Makes about 3 cups.

Friendly Ghost Cupcakes

- 1⅓ cups all-purpose flour
- ¾ cup unsweetened cocoa powder
- 2 teaspoons baking powder
- ½ teaspoon salt
- ¼ teaspoon baking soda
- 1 cup sugar
- 6 tablespoons (¾ stick) unsalted butter, softened
- 1 cup sugar
- 2 eggs
- 1 teaspoon vanilla
- ¾ cup milk
- 1 cup prepared chocolate frosting
- 4 cups whipped topping
- Mini semisweet chocolate chips

1. Preheat oven to 350°F. Line 14 standard (2½-inch) muffin cups with paper baking cups.

2. Whisk flour, cocoa powder, baking powder, salt and baking soda in medium bowl. Beat sugar and butter in large bowl with electric mixer at medium speed until fluffy. Add eggs and vanilla; beat until well blended. Add flour mixture and milk; beat at low speed just until combined. Spoon batter evenly into prepared muffin cups.

3. Bake 15 minutes or until toothpick inserted into centers comes out clean. Cool in pans 10 minutes. Remove to wire racks; cool completely.

4. Place frosting in medium microwavable bowl; microwave on HIGH 10 seconds. Stir; microwave 10 seconds or just until melted. Working with one at a time, hold cupcake upside down and dip top into melted frosting; tilt cupcake to let excess frosting drip off. Return to wire rack; let stand until frosting is set.

5. Place whipped topping in pastry bag or resealable food storage bag with 1 inch cut off one corner of bag. Pipe ghost shape onto each cupcake (or drop whipped topping by spoonfuls onto cupcakes to resemble ghosts); add chocolate chips for eyes. Refrigerate until ready to serve.

Makes 14 cupcakes

Carrot Cake Minis

- 1 cup packed light brown sugar
- ¾ cup plus 2 tablespoons all-purpose flour
- 1 teaspoon baking soda
- ½ teaspoon salt
- ½ teaspoon ground cinnamon
- ¼ teaspoon ground nutmeg
- ⅛ teaspoon ground cloves
- ½ cup canola oil
- 2 eggs
- 1½ cups lightly packed grated carrots
- ½ teaspoon vanilla
- Cream Cheese Frosting (recipe follows)
- Toasted shredded coconut (optional)

1. Preheat oven to 350°F. Line 36 mini (1¾-inch) muffin cups with paper baking cups.

2. Whisk brown sugar, flour, baking soda, salt, cinnamon, nutmeg and cloves in large bowl. Stir in oil. Add eggs, one at a time, stirring until blended after each addition. Stir in carrots and vanilla. Spoon batter evenly into prepared muffin cups.

3. Bake 15 minutes or until toothpick inserted into centers comes out clean. Cool in pans 5 minutes. Remove to wire racks; cool completely.

4. Meanwhile, prepare Cream Cheese Frosting. Frost cupcakes. Sprinkle with toasted coconut, if desired. Cover and store in refrigerator.

Makes 36 mini cupcakes

Cream Cheese Frosting: Beat 1 package (8 ounces) softened cream cheese and ¼ cup (½ stick) softened unsalted butter in medium bowl with electric mixer at medium-high speed until creamy. Gradually beat in 1½ cups sifted powdered sugar until well blended. Beat in ¼ teaspoon salt and ¼ teaspoon vanilla. Makes about 3 cups.

Tip

You can use your food processor to quickly grate the carrots for this recipe. Use the metal blade and pulse the carrots until they are evenly grated.

Scarecrow Cupcakes

1¼ cups all-purpose flour
¾ teaspoon baking powder
½ teaspoon baking soda
¼ teaspoon salt
¾ teaspoon ground cinnamon
⅛ teaspoon ground cloves
⅛ teaspoon ground nutmeg
⅛ teaspoon ground allspice
¾ cup whipping cream
2 tablespoons molasses
¼ cup (½ stick) butter, softened
¼ cup granulated sugar
¼ cup packed brown sugar
2 eggs
½ teaspoon vanilla
¾ cup shredded coconut
Simple Fall Frosting (recipe follows)
Gumdrop Hats (recipe follows)
Toasted coconut, chow mein noodles, shredded wheat cereal, assorted candies and decorating gel

1. Preheat oven to 350°F. Line 18 standard (2½-inch) muffin cups with paper baking cups. Combine flour, baking powder, baking soda, salt and spices in medium bowl. Combine cream and molasses in small bowl.

2. Beat butter in large bowl with electric mixer at medium speed until creamy. Add granulated sugar and brown sugar; beat until light and fluffy. Add eggs, one at a time, beating well after each addition. Blend in vanilla.

3. Add flour mixture alternately with cream mixture, beating well after each addition. Stir in coconut. Spoon batter into prepared muffin cups, filling about half full.

4. Bake 20 minutes or until toothpick inserted into centers comes out clean. Cool in pans 10 minutes. Remove to wire racks; cool completely.

5. Prepare Simple Fall Frosting and Gumdrop Hats. Frost cupcakes and decorate to create scarecrow faces.

Makes 18 cupcakes

Simple Fall Frosting: Beat 2 tablespoons softened butter and 2 tablespoons maple syrup in medium bowl until blended. Gradually beat in 1½ cups powdered sugar until smooth. Makes about 1 cup.

Gumdrop Hats: Roll out a large gumdrop on a generously sugared surface. Cut one rounded piece for the top of the hat and one straight piece for the brim of the hat as shown in the photo. Overlap the pieces to make the hat; pipe decorating gel over the seam for the hat band.

Glazed Applesauce Spice Cupcakes

- 1 cup packed light brown sugar
- ¾ cup (1½ sticks) unsalted butter, softened
- 3 eggs
- 1½ teaspoons vanilla
- 2¼ cups all-purpose flour
- 2 teaspoons baking soda
- 2 teaspoons ground cinnamon
- ¾ teaspoon ground nutmeg
- ½ teaspoon ground ginger
- ¼ teaspoon salt
- 1½ cups unsweetened applesauce
- ½ cup milk
- ⅔ cup chopped walnuts, plus additional for garnish
- ⅔ cup butterscotch chips, plus additional for garnish
- Apple Glaze (recipe follows)

1. Preheat oven to 350°F. Line 24 standard (2½-inch) muffin cups with paper baking cups.

2. Beat brown sugar and butter in large bowl with electric mixer at medium speed until light and fluffy. Beat in eggs and vanilla until well blended.

3. Whisk flour, baking soda, cinnamon, nutmeg, ginger and salt in medium bowl. Add one third of flour mixture to butter mixture; beat until blended. Add milk; beat until blended. Alternately add remaining flour mixture and applesauce, beating well after each addition. Stir in walnuts and butterscotch chips. Spoon batter evenly into prepared muffin cups.

4. Bake 15 minutes or until toothpick inserted into centers comes out clean. Cool in pans 10 minutes. Remove to wire racks; cool completely. Meanwhile, prepare Apple Glaze.

5. Pour Apple Glaze over cupcakes. Let stand 5 minutes or until glaze is set. Sprinkle with additional walnuts and butterscotch chips.

Makes 24 cupcakes

Apple Glaze: Place 1 cup sifted powdered sugar in small bowl. Stir in 2 to 3 tablespoons apple juice concentrate to make stiff glaze. Makes about 1 cup.

Black Cat Cupcakes

1 package (about 18 ounces) cake mix, any flavor, plus ingredients to prepare mix
1 container (16 ounces) chocolate fudge frosting
White decorating icing
Graham crackers, cut into small triangles
Black string licorice
Assorted candies

1. Preheat oven to 350°F. Line 24 standard (2½-inch) muffin cups with paper baking cups.

2. Prepare cake mix according to package directions. Spoon batter into prepared muffin cups, filling two-thirds full.

3. Bake 20 minutes or until toothpick inserted into centers comes out clean. Cool in pans 10 minutes. Remove to wire racks; cool completely.

4. Frost cupcakes. Pipe two mounds of frosting in center of each cupcake for cheeks. Pipe mouths using decorating icing. Press graham cracker triangles into cupcakes for ears. Decorate cat faces with licorice and assorted candies. *Makes 24 cupcakes*

Polka Dot Pumpkin Cupcakes

½ cup (4 ounces) cream cheese, softened
1 large egg
2 tablespoons granulated sugar
⅔ cup NESTLÉ® TOLL HOUSE® Semi-Sweet Chocolate Mini Morsels
1 package (16 ounces) pound cake mix
1 cup LIBBY'S® 100% Pure Pumpkin
⅓ cup water
2 large eggs
2 teaspoons pumpkin pie spice
1 teaspoon baking soda

PREHEAT oven to 325°F. Grease or paper-line 18 muffin cups.

BEAT cream cheese, egg and granulated sugar in small mixer bowl until smooth. Stir in morsels. Set aside.

COMBINE cake mix, pumpkin, water, eggs, pumpkin pie spice and baking soda in large mixer bowl; beat on medium speed for 3 minutes. Pour batter into prepared muffin cups, filling ¾ full. Spoon about 1 tablespoon topping over batter in each muffin cup.

BAKE for 25 to 30 minutes or until wooden pick inserted in centers comes out clean. Cool in pans on wire racks for 10 minutes; remove to wire racks to cool completely.
Makes 18 cupcakes

Prep Time: 15 minutes
Cook Time: 25 minutes
Cooling Time: 10 minutes

Black Cat Cupcakes

Cappuccino Cupcakes

- 1 package (about 18 ounces) dark chocolate cake mix
- 1⅓ cups strong brewed or instant coffee, at room temperature
- 3 eggs
- ⅓ cup vegetable oil or melted butter
- 1 container (16 ounces) vanilla frosting
- 2 tablespoons coffee liqueur
- Additional coffee liqueur (optional)
- Grated chocolate*
- Chocolate-covered coffee beans (optional)

**Grate half of a 3- or 4-ounce milk, dark or espresso chocolate bar on the large holes of a grater.*

1. Preheat oven to 350°F. Line 24 standard (2½-inch) muffin cups with foil or paper baking cups.

2. Beat cake mix, coffee, eggs and oil in large bowl with electric mixer at low speed 30 seconds. Beat at medium speed 2 minutes. Spoon batter into prepared muffin cups, filling two-thirds full.

3. Bake 20 minutes or until toothpick inserted into centers comes out clean. Cool in pans 10 minutes. Remove to wire racks; cool completely.

4. Combine frosting and 2 tablespoons liqueur in small bowl; mix well. Poke about 10 holes in each cupcake with toothpick. Pour 1 to 2 teaspoons additional liqueur over top of each cupcake, if desired. Frost cupcakes; sprinkle with grated chocolate. Garnish with chocolate-covered coffee beans. *Makes 24 cupcakes*

Tip: Cupcakes are the perfect party treat because they can often be made ahead of time. These cupcakes can be tightly wrapped and frozen for up to 3 months after baking. Thaw at room temperature before frosting.

Taffy Apple Cupcakes

1¾ cups all-purpose flour
1 teaspoon baking soda
1 teaspoon ground cinnamon
½ teaspoon salt
1 cup applesauce
¾ cup sugar
½ cup vegetable oil
1 egg
1 package (14 ounces) caramels
3 tablespoons milk
10 wooden craft sticks
¾ cup chopped roasted peanuts

1. Preheat oven to 350°F. Spray 30 mini (1¾-inch) muffin cups with nonstick cooking spray or line with paper baking cups.

2. Whisk flour, baking soda, cinnamon and salt in medium bowl. Combine applesauce, sugar, oil and egg in large bowl. Add flour mixture; stir until blended. Spoon batter into prepared muffin cups, filling three-fourths full.

3. Bake 15 minutes or until toothpick inserted into centers comes out clean. Cool in pans 5 minutes. Remove to wire racks; cool completely.

4. Line baking sheet with waxed paper; spray with nonstick cooking spray. Place peanuts on plate or in shallow dish. Insert craft sticks into tops of 10 cupcakes. (Reserve remaining cupcakes for another use.)

5. Place unwrapped caramels and milk in large microwavable bowl; microwave on HIGH 2 to 3 minutes or until melted and smooth, stirring after each minute. Working with one at a time, hold cupcake over bowl and spoon caramel over cupcake, rotating until completely coated. Immediately roll in peanuts to coat, pressing to adhere. Stand cupcake on prepared baking sheet. (Caramel may need to be reheated briefly if it becomes too thick.) Let stand 20 minutes or until set.

Makes 30 mini cupcakes (10 with caramel and 20 plain)

Note: To make all 30 cupcakes into Taffy Apple Cupcakes, use three packages of caramels and ½ cup milk. For a quicker version of the recipe, simply drizzle melted caramel over the cooled cupcakes and sprinkle with chopped peanuts.

Halloween Hedgehogs

- 1 package (about 18 ounces) chocolate cake mix, plus ingredients to prepare mix
- 1 container (16 ounces) chocolate frosting
- White chocolate chips
- Black jelly beans, cut into halves
- Black decorating gel (optional)
- 3 cups candy corn

1. Preheat oven to 350°F. Line 22 standard (2½-inch) muffin cups with paper baking cups. Prepare cake mix according to package directions. Spoon batter into prepared muffin cups, filling two-thirds full.

2. Bake 20 minutes or until toothpick inserted into centers comes out clean. Cool in pans 10 minutes. Remove to wire racks; cool completely.

3. Frost cupcakes. Cut jelly beans in half crosswise for noses. Arrange white chips and jelly bean half on one side of each cupcake to create face; pipe dot of frosting or decorating gel onto each eye. Arrange candy corn around face and all over each cupcake.

Makes 22 cupcakes

Touchdown Brownie Cups

- 1 cup (2 sticks) butter or margarine
- ½ cup HERSHEY'S Cocoa or HERSHEY'S SPECIAL DARK® Cocoa
- 1 cup packed light brown sugar
- ½ cup granulated sugar
- 3 eggs
- 1 teaspoon vanilla extract
- 1 cup all-purpose flour
- 1⅓ cups chopped pecans, divided

1. Heat oven to 350°F. Line 2½-inch muffin cups with foil or paper bake cups.

2. Place butter in large microwave-safe bowl; cover. Microwave at MEDIUM (50%) 1½ minutes or until melted. Add cocoa; stir until smooth. Add brown sugar and granulated sugar; stir until well blended. Add eggs and vanilla; beat well. Add flour and 1 cup pecans; stir until well blended. Fill prepared muffin cups about three-fourths full of batter; sprinkle about 1 teaspoon remaining pecans over top of each.

3. Bake 20 to 25 minutes or until tops begin to dry and crack. Cool completely in cups on wire rack.

Makes about 17 cupcakes

Halloween Hedgehogs

Peanut Butter & Jelly Cupcakes

- 1 package (about 18 ounces) yellow cake mix, plus ingredients to prepare mix
- 2 cups strawberry jelly
- ¾ cup creamy peanut butter
- ½ cup (1 stick) butter, softened
- 2 cups powdered sugar
- ½ teaspoon vanilla
- ¼ cup milk

1. Preheat oven to 350°F. Line 22 standard (2½-inch) muffin cups with paper baking cups. Prepare cake mix according to package directions. Spoon batter into prepared muffin cups, filling two-thirds full.

2. Bake 20 minutes or until toothpick inserted into centers comes out clean. Cool in pans 10 minutes. Remove to wire racks; cool completely.

3. Fill pastry bag fitted with small round tip with jelly. Insert tip into top of cupcake; squeeze bag gently to fill center of cupcake with jelly. (Stop squeezing when you feel resistance or jelly comes out of top of cupcake.) Repeat with remaining cupcakes and jelly.

4. Beat peanut butter and butter in medium bowl with electric mixer at medium speed 2 minutes or until smooth. Add powdered sugar and vanilla; beat at low speed 1 minute or until crumbly. Slowly add milk, beating until creamy. Pipe or spread onto cupcakes.

Makes 22 cupcakes

Mummy Cakes

- 1 package (about 18 ounces) chocolate cake mix, plus ingredients to prepare mix
- ¼ cup plus 3 tablespoons unsweetened cocoa powder, divided
- 1 teaspoon ground cinnamon
- 1 teaspoon ground ginger
- 1 package (about 16 ounces) refrigerated sugar cookie dough, softened
- 4 cups powdered sugar
- ⅓ cup plus 1 tablespoon milk
- 2 teaspoons butter, softened
- 48 small red cinnamon candies
- ½ cup chocolate cookie crumbs

1. Preheat oven to 350°F. Line 24 standard (2½-inch) muffin cups with paper baking cups. Prepare cake mix according to package directions. Spoon batter into prepared muffin cups, filling two-thirds full.

2. Bake 20 minutes or until toothpick inserted into centers comes out clean. Cool in pans 10 minutes. Remove to wire racks; cool completely.

3. Knead ¼ cup cocoa, cinnamon and ginger into cookie dough on lightly floured work surface until well blended. Roll out dough to ¼-inch thickness. Cut out shapes using 3-inch gingerbread man cookie cutter; place on ungreased cookie sheets. Bake 7 minutes or until edges are set. Remove to wire racks; cool completely.

4. Beat powdered sugar, milk and butter in large bowl with electric mixer at medium speed until creamy. Spoon about one third of frosting into 1-quart resealable food storage bag with small tip cut from one corner. Adhere two cinnamon candies to face of each cookie for eyes using small dots of frosting. Pipe frosting across cookies for mummy wrappings. Let stand until frosting is set.

5. Add remaining 3 tablespoons cocoa to remaining white frosting; stir until blended. Pipe or spread onto cupcakes; sprinkle with cookie crumbs. Gently push one mummy cookie into each cupcake at an angle.

Makes 24 cupcakes

Pecan Tassies

- 4 ounces (½ of 8-ounce package) PHILADELPHIA® Cream Cheese, softened
- ½ cup (1 stick) butter or margarine, softened
- 1 cup all-purpose flour
- 1 egg
- ¾ cup firmly packed brown sugar
- 1 teaspoon vanilla
- ¾ cup finely chopped PLANTERS® Pecans
- 3 squares BAKER'S® Semi-Sweet Baking Chocolate, melted

BEAT cream cheese and butter in large bowl with electric mixer on medium speed until well blended. Add flour; mix well. Cover and refrigerate at least 1 hour or until chilled.

PREHEAT oven to 350°F. Divide dough into 24 balls. Place 1 ball in each of 24 miniature muffin pan cups; press onto bottoms and up sides of cups to form shells. Set aside. Beat egg lightly in small bowl. Add sugar and vanilla; mix well. Stir in pecans. Spoon evenly into pastry shells, filling each shell three-fourths full.

BAKE 25 minutes or until lightly browned. Let stand 5 minutes in pans; remove to wire racks. Cool completely. Drizzle with melted chocolate. Let stand until set.

Makes 24 servings

Prep Time: 20 minutes plus refrigerating
Bake Time: 25 minutes

Tip

Pecans, a member of the hickory family, are native to the United States. They are widely grown in Georgia, Oklahoma and Texas. The nut has a smooth tan shell which is thin, but hard. The flesh is beige with a thin brown exterior. These nuts are widely eaten out of hand and used in a variety of sweet and savory dishes.

Feathered Friends

1 package (19 to 20 ounces) brownie mix for 13×9-inch pan, plus ingredients to prepare mix

72 red, orange and/or yellow gummy fish candies

1½ containers (16 ounces each) chocolate frosting

White decorating icing

Mini semisweet chocolate chips

1. Preheat oven to 350°F. Line 12 standard (2½-inch) muffin cups with paper baking cups. Prepare brownie mix according to package directions for cake-like brownies. Spoon batter evenly into prepared muffin cups.

2. Bake 24 minutes or until toothpick inserted into centers comes out clean. Cool in pan 10 minutes. Remove to wire rack; cool completely.

3. Use sharp knife to cut gummy fish in half lengthwise and create two thinner fish. Cut tails off of each fish; reserve tails.

4. Frost cupcakes. Arrange 12 gummy fish halves, cut sides facing up, in two rows on one side of each cupcake, pressing cut ends of fish into cupcake as shown in photo.

5. Place remaining frosting in pastry bag or resealable food storage bag with hole cut in one corner of bag. Pipe 1½-inch mound of frosting on opposite side of each cupcake to create head. Pipe eyes with decorating icing; place mini chocolate chip in center of each eye. Use reserved gummy fish tails to create beaks. Set cupcakes on gummy fish tails to resemble feet, if desired.

Makes 12 cupcakes

Caramel Apple Cupcakes

- 1 package (about 18 ounces) butter recipe yellow cake mix, plus ingredients to prepare mix
- 1 cup chopped dried apples
- Caramel Frosting (recipe follows)
- Chopped pecans

1. Preheat oven to 375°F. Line 24 standard (2½-inch) muffin cups with paper baking cups.
2. Prepare cake mix according to package directions; stir in apples. Spoon batter into prepared muffin cups, filling two-thirds full.
3. Bake 20 minutes or until toothpick inserted into centers comes out clean. Cool in pans 10 minutes. Remove to wire racks; cool completely.
4. Prepare Caramel Frosting. Frost cupcakes; sprinkle with pecans.

Makes 24 cupcakes

Caramel Frosting

- 3 tablespoons butter
- 1 cup packed light brown sugar
- ½ cup evaporated milk
- ⅛ teaspoon salt
- 3¾ cups powdered sugar
- ¾ teaspoon vanilla

1. Melt butter in medium saucepan. Stir in brown sugar, evaporated milk and salt. Bring to a boil, stirring constantly. Remove from heat; cool slightly.
2. Add powdered sugar; beat with electric mixer at medium speed until frosting reaches desired spreading consistency. Add vanilla; beat until smooth.

Makes about 3 cups

Mini Doughnut Cupcakes

- 1 cup sugar
- 1½ teaspoons ground cinnamon
- 1 package (about 18 ounces) yellow or white cake mix, plus ingredients to prepare mix
- 1 tablespoon ground nutmeg

1. Preheat oven to 350°F. Grease and flour 60 mini (1¾-inch) muffin cups. Combine sugar and cinnamon in small bowl; set aside.

2. Prepare cake mix according to package directions; stir in nutmeg. Spoon batter into prepared muffin cups, filling two-thirds full.

3. Bake 10 minutes or until lightly browned and toothpick inserted into centers comes out clean.

4. Remove cupcakes from pans. Roll warm cupcakes in sugar mixture until completely coated. *Makes 60 mini cupcakes*

Note: Save any remaining sugar mixture to sprinkle on toast and pancakes.

Graveyard Cupcakes

- 24 Pepperidge Farm® MILANO®, MINI MILANO®, and BRUSSELS® Distinctive Cookies *or* Home Style Sugar Cookies
- 4 tubes (4.25 ounces *each*) decorating icing *or* 4 tubes (.68 ounces *each* decorating gel (black white, orange *and* green)
- Orange-colored sugar crystals
- 24 store-purchased frosted cupcakes

DECORATE MILANO® cookies using black and white icing or gel to resemble tombstones and ghosts.

DECORATE BRUSSELS® or Sugar cookies using orange and green icing or gel and sugar crystals to resemble pumpkins and spider webs.

PLACE decorated cookies into tops of cupcakes.

Makes 24 servings

Prep Time: 20 minutes

Mini Doughnut Cupcakes

Double Malted Cupcakes

Cupcakes

- 2 cups all-purpose flour
- ¼ cup malted milk powder
- 2 teaspoons baking powder
- ¼ teaspoon salt
- 1¾ cups granulated sugar
- ½ cup (1 stick) butter, softened
- 1 cup milk
- 1½ teaspoons vanilla
- 3 egg whites

Frosting

- 4 ounces milk chocolate candy bar, broken into chunks
- ¼ cup (½ stick) butter
- ¼ cup whipping cream
- 1 tablespoon malted milk powder
- 1 teaspoon vanilla
- 1¾ cups powdered sugar
- 30 chocolate-covered malt ball candies

1. Preheat oven to 350°F. Line 30 standard (2½-inch) muffin cups with paper baking cups.

2. For cupcakes, whisk flour, ¼ cup malted milk powder, baking powder and salt in medium bowl. Beat granulated sugar and ½ cup butter in large bowl with electric mixer at medium speed 1 minute. Add milk and 1½ teaspoons vanilla; beat at low speed 30 seconds. Gradually beat in flour mixture; beat at medium speed 2 minutes. Add egg whites; beat 1 minute. Spoon batter into prepared muffin cups, filling two-thirds full.

3. Bake 20 minutes or until toothpick inserted into centers comes out clean. Cool in pans 10 minutes. (Centers of cupcakes will sink slightly upon cooling.) Remove to wire racks; cool completely.

4. For frosting, melt chocolate and ¼ cup butter in heavy medium saucepan over low heat, stirring frequently. Stir in cream, 1 tablespoon malted milk powder and 1 teaspoon vanilla. Gradually stir in powdered sugar. Cook and stir constantly until smooth. Remove from heat. Refrigerate 20 minutes, beating every 5 minutes or until frosting is spreadable.

5. Frost cupcakes; decorate with malt ball candies. Store at room temperature up to 24 hours or cover and refrigerate for up to 3 days.

Makes 30 cupcakes

Spider Web Pull-Apart Cake

- 1 package (9 ounces) yellow cake mix
- Red and yellow food coloring
- 1 container (16 ounces) lemon or vanilla frosting
- 1 tube (about 4 ounces) black decorating icing
- 1 black licorice stick
- 1 small chocolate wafer cookie
- 2 mini marshmallows

1. Preheat oven to 350°F. Line 12 standard (2½-inch) muffin cups with paper baking cups. Prepare cake mix according to package directions. Spoon batter into prepared muffin cups, filling two-thirds full.

2. Bake 20 minutes or until toothpick inserted into centers comes out clean. Cool in pans 10 minutes. Remove to wire racks; cool completely. Use seven cupcakes for recipe; reserve five cupcakes for another use.

3. Place one cupcake in center of serving platter; arrange remaining six cupcakes around it.

4. Tint frosting with food coloring to desired shade of orange. Drop frosting by large spoonfuls onto each cupcake. Spread over cupcakes.

5. Starting in center, pipe decorating icing in spiral pattern. Use toothpick or small knife to draw lines from center to outer edge of cupcakes to create web pattern.

6. Cut licorice stick into eight pieces. Place licorice pieces in two rows of four on one end of web for spider legs. Top with cookie. Dot icing on bottom of each marshmallow; place on cookie. Pipe small dots of icing on marshmallow tops for eyes.

Makes 7 servings

Cookies & Cream Cupcakes

- 2¼ cups all-purpose flour
- 1 tablespoon baking powder
- ½ teaspoon salt
- 1⅔ cups sugar
- 1 cup milk
- ½ cup (1 stick) butter, softened
- 2 teaspoons vanilla
- 3 egg whites
- 1 cup crushed chocolate sandwich cookies (about 10 cookies), plus additional for garnish
- 1 container (16 ounces) vanilla frosting

1. Preheat oven to 350°F. Lightly grease 24 standard (2½-inch) muffin cups or line with paper baking cups.

2. Sift flour, baking powder and salt into large bowl. Stir in sugar. Add milk, butter and vanilla; beat with electric mixer at low speed 30 seconds. Beat at medium speed 2 minutes. Add egg whites; beat 2 minutes. Stir in 1 cup crushed cookies. Spoon batter into prepared muffin cups, filling two-thirds full.

3. Bake 20 minutes or until toothpick inserted into centers comes out clean. Cool in pans 10 minutes. Remove to wire racks; cool completely.

4. Frost cupcakes; garnish with additional crushed cookies.

Makes 24 cupcakes

Toffee Bits Cheesecake Cups

- About 16 to 18 vanilla wafer cookies
- 3 packages (8 ounces each) cream cheese, softened
- ¾ cup sugar
- 3 eggs
- 1 teaspoon vanilla extract
- 1⅓ cups (8-ounce package) HEATH® BITS 'O BRICKLE® Toffee Bits, divided

1. Heat oven to 350°F. Line 2½-inch muffin cups with foil bake cups; place vanilla wafer on bottom of each cup.

2. Beat cream cheese and sugar in large bowl on low speed of mixer until smooth. Beat in eggs and vanilla just until blended. Do not overbeat. Gently stir 1 cup toffee bits into batter; pour into prepared cups to ¼ inch from top.

3. Bake 20 to 25 minutes or until almost set. Remove from oven. Immediately sprinkle about ½ teaspoon toffee bits onto each cup. Cool completely in pan on wire rack. Remove from pan. Cover; refrigerate about 3 hours. Store leftover cups in refrigerator.

Makes about 16 to 18 cups

Cookies & Cream Cupcakes

Sweet Potato Spice Cupcakes

- 1¼ pounds sweet potatoes, quartered
- 1½ cups all-purpose flour
- 1¼ cups granulated sugar
- 2 teaspoons baking powder
- 1 teaspoon ground cinnamon
- ½ teaspoon baking soda
- ½ teaspoon salt
- ¼ teaspoon ground allspice
- ¾ cup canola or vegetable oil
- 2 eggs
- ½ cup chopped walnuts or pecans, plus additional for garnish
- ½ cup raisins
- Cream Cheese Frosting (recipe follows)

1. Place sweet potatoes in large saucepan; add 1 inch water. Cover and cook over medium heat 30 minutes or until fork-tender, adding additional water, if necessary. Drain potatoes; peel and mash when cool enough to handle.

2. Preheat oven to 325°F. Line 18 standard (2½-inch) muffin cups with paper baking cups.

3. Whisk flour, granulated sugar, baking powder, cinnamon, baking soda, salt and allspice in medium bowl. Beat mashed sweet potato (about 2 cups), oil and eggs in large bowl with electric mixer at low speed until blended. Add flour mixture; beat at medium speed 30 seconds or until well blended. Stir in ½ cup walnuts and raisins. Spoon batter evenly into prepared muffin cups.

4. Bake 20 minutes or until toothpick inserted into centers comes out clean. Cool completely in pans on wire rack.

5. Meanwhile, prepare Cream Cheese Frosting. Frost cupcakes; sprinkle with additional walnuts. Cover and store in refrigerator.

Makes 18 cupcakes

Cream Cheese Frosting: Beat 1 package (8 ounces) softened cream cheese and ¼ cup (½ stick) softened unsalted butter in medium bowl with electric mixer at medium-high speed until creamy. Gradually beat in 1½ cups sifted powdered sugar until well blended. Beat in ¼ teaspoon salt and ¼ teaspoon vanilla. Makes about 3 cups.

Winter Wonderland

Snowy Peaks

- 1 package (about 18 ounces) chocolate cake mix, plus ingredients to prepare mix
- 4 egg whites, at room temperature
- 6 tablespoons sugar

1. Preheat oven to 350°F. Line 9 jumbo (3½-inch) muffin cups with paper baking cups. Prepare cake mix according to package directions. Spoon batter into prepared muffin cups, filling two-thirds full.
2. Bake 23 to 25 minutes or until toothpick inserted into centers comes out clean. Cool in pans 10 minutes. Remove to wire racks; cool completely. *Increase oven temperature to 375°F.*
3. Beat egg whites in medium bowl with electric mixer at high speed until soft peaks form. Continue beating while gradually adding sugar; beat until stiff peaks form. Pipe or spread meringue on each cupcake.
4. Place cupcakes on baking sheet. Bake 5 minutes or until peaks of meringue are golden.

Makes 9 jumbo cupcakes

Wigglin' Jigglin' Cupcakes

2½ cups boiling water (Do not add cold water)
2 packages (8-serving size each) JELL-O® Cherry Flavor Gelatin
1 package (2-layer size) yellow cake mix
1 tub (8 ounces) COOL WHIP® Whipped Topping, thawed
Holiday sprinkles

STIR boiling water into dry gelatin mix in medium bowl at least 3 minutes until completely dissolved. Pour into 15×10×1-inch pan.

REFRIGERATE at least 3 hours or until firm. Meanwhile, prepare and bake cake mix as directed on package for 24 cupcakes. Cool completely on wire racks. Cut each cupcake in half horizontally.

DIP bottom of 15×10×1-inch pan in warm water about 15 seconds. Using 2-inch round cookie cutter, cut out 24 JIGGLERS. Place a small dollop of whipped topping on bottom half of each cupcake; top with JIGGLERS circle and another small dollop of whipped topping. Place top half of cupcake on each stack; press gently into whipped topping. Top with the remaining whipped topping and sprinkles.

Makes 24 cupcakes

Jazz It Up: Gently stir a few drops of food coloring into whipped topping before spreading on the cupcakes.

Prep Time: 45 minutes
Total time: 3 hours 45 minutes (includes refrigerating)

Chocolate Sweetheart Cupcakes

- 1 package (about 18 ounces) dark chocolate cake mix, plus ingredients to prepare mix
- 1 container (16 ounces) vanilla frosting
- 3 tablespoons seedless raspberry jam

1. Preheat oven to 350°F. Line 24 standard (2½-inch) muffin cups with paper baking cups. Prepare cake mix according to package directions. Spoon batter into prepared muffin cups, filling two-thirds full.

2. Bake 20 minutes or until toothpick inserted into centers comes out clean. Cool in pans 10 minutes. Remove to wire racks; cool completely.

3. Combine frosting and jam in medium bowl. Cut off rounded tops of cupcakes with serrated knife. Cut out heart shape from each cupcake top with mini cookie cutter.

4. Spread frosting mixture generously over cupcake bottoms, mounding slightly in center. Replace cupcake tops, pressing gently to fill hearts with frosting mixture. *Makes 24 cupcakes*

Snowy Owl Cupcakes

- 1 package (about 18 ounces) white cake mix, plus ingredients to prepare mix
- 1 container (16 ounces) vanilla frosting
- 2½ cups shredded coconut
- 48 gummy candy rings
- Black decorating gel
- 24 black jelly beans

1. Preheat oven to 350°F. Line 24 standard (2½-inch) muffin cups with paper baking cups or spray with nonstick cooking spray. Prepare cake mix according to package directions. Spoon batter into prepared muffin cups, filling two-thirds full.

2. Bake 20 minutes or until toothpick inserted into centers comes out clean. Cool in pans 10 minutes. Remove to wire racks; cool completely.

3. Frost cupcakes. Sprinkle coconut over each cupcake, covering completely. Place two gummy rings on each cupcake for eyes; pipe dots in centers with decorating gel. Place jelly bean in center of each cupcake for beak. *Makes 24 cupcakes*

Chocolate Sweetheart Cupcakes

Zesty Orange Cookie Cups

- 1 cup (2 sticks) butter, softened
- ½ cup granulated sugar
- 2 cups all-purpose flour
- 2 cups (12-ounce package) NESTLÉ® TOLL HOUSE® Premier White Morsels
- 2 large eggs
- 1 can (14 ounces) NESTLÉ® CARNATION® Sweetened Condensed Milk
- ½ to ¾ teaspoon orange extract
- 1 tablespoon grated orange peel (1 medium orange)

PREHEAT oven to 350°F. Grease 48 mini muffin cups.

BEAT butter and sugar in medium mixer bowl until creamy. Add flour; beat until mixture is evenly moistened, crumbly and can be formed into balls. Shape dough into 1-inch balls. Press each ball onto bottom and up side of prepared muffin cups to form wells. Place 5 morsels in each cup.

BEAT eggs in medium bowl with wire whisk. Stir in sweetened condensed milk and orange extract. Spoon almost a measuring tablespoon of mixture into each muffin cup, filling about ¾ full.

BAKE for 15 to 17 minutes or until centers are puffed and edges are just beginning to brown. Upon removing from oven, gently run knife around each cup. **While still warm,** top each cup with 8 to 10 morsels (they will soften and retain their shape). Cool completely in pans on wire racks. With tip of knife, remove cookie cups from muffin pans. Top with grated orange peel just before serving. Store in covered container in refrigerator.

Makes 48 cookie cups

Sweet Snowmen

1 package (about 18 ounces) vanilla cake mix, plus ingredients to prepare mix
1 container (16 ounces) white frosting
22 standard marshmallows
1 package (7 ounces) flaked coconut
44 large black gumdrops
Mini orange candy-coated chocolate pieces
Mini semisweet chocolate chips
Round green gummy candies
Red pull-apart licorice twists

1. Preheat oven to 350°F. Line 22 standard (2½-inch) muffin cups with paper baking cups. Prepare cake mix according to package directions. Spoon batter into prepared muffin cups, filling two-thirds full.

2. Bake 20 minutes or until toothpick inserted into centers comes out clean. Cool in pans 10 minutes. Remove to wire racks; cool completely.

3. Frost cupcakes. Place 1 marshmallow on each cupcake for head, arranging slightly off center. Lightly press coconut into frosting around marshmallow.

4. For each hat, press 1 gumdrop on countertop or between hands to flatten into 2-inch circle. Attach second gumdrop to center of flattened gumdrop with small dab of frosting.

5. Cut chocolate pieces in half with sharp knife. Decorate snowmen with chocolate chips for eyes, chocolate pieces for noses and gummy candies for buttons, attaching with frosting. Separate licorice twists into 2-string pieces; cut into 6- to 8-inch lengths and tie around bottom of marshmallows to create scarves. Attach hats to tops of marshmallows with frosting. *Makes 22 cupcakes*

Chocolate Cheesecakes For Two

- 2 ounces (¼ of 8-ounce package) PHILADELPHIA® Cream Cheese, softened
- 1 tablespoon sugar
- 1 square BAKER'S® Semi-Sweet Baking Chocolate, melted
- ½ cup thawed COOL WHIP® Whipped Topping
- 2 OREO® Chocolate Sandwich Cookies

BEAT cream cheese, sugar and chocolate in medium bowl with wire whisk until well blended. Add whipped topping; mix well.

PLACE 1 cookie on bottom of each of 2 paper-lined medium muffin cups; fill evenly with cream cheese mixture.

REFRIGERATE 2 hours or overnight. (Or, if you are in a hurry, place in the freezer for 1 hour.) *Makes 2 servings*

Jazz It Up: Dust surface with cocoa powder. Top with heart-shaped stencil; dust with powdered sugar.

Prep Time: 10 minutes plus refrigerating

I Think You're "Marbleous" Cupcakes

- 1 package (about 18 ounces) cake mix with pudding in the mix, any flavor
- 1¼ cups water
- 3 eggs
- ¼ cup vegetable oil
- 1 container (16 ounces) vanilla frosting
- 1 tube (about 4 ounces) red decorating gel

1. Preheat oven to 350°F. Grease 24 standard (2½-inch) muffin cups or line with paper baking cups.
2. Prepare cake mix according to package directions using water, eggs and oil. Spoon batter into prepared muffin cups, filling two-thirds full.
3. Bake 20 minutes or until toothpick inserted into centers comes out clean. Cool in pans 10 minutes. Remove to wire racks; cool completely.
4. Spread frosting over each cupcake. Fit round decorating tip onto tube of decorating gel. Squeeze 5 dots of gel on each cupcake. Swirl toothpick through gel and frosting in continuous motion to make marbleized pattern or heart shapes.

Makes 24 cupcakes

Mini Fruitcake Cupcakes

- 1½ cups dried fruit (raisins, cherries, cranberries, dates, chopped figs or apricots)
- ½ cup Port wine or orange juice
- ⅓ cup granulated sugar
- 5 tablespoons unsalted butter
- ¼ cup light brown sugar
- 2 eggs
- 2 tablespoons orange juice
- 1 teaspoon finely grated orange peel
- ¾ cup all-purpose flour
- ½ teaspoon *each* baking powder, ground ginger and ground cinnamon
- ¼ teaspoon *each* salt and ground allspice
- ½ cup chopped pecans, toasted
- 1 cup powdered sugar
- 3 tablespoons lemon juice

1. Preheat oven to 350°F. Spray 28 mini (1¾-inch) muffin cups with nonstick cooking spray or line with paper baking cups.

2. Combine dried fruits and Port wine in medium microwavable bowl. Cover; microwave on HIGH 1 minute. Stir; microwave 1 minute. Let stand 15 minutes or until cool.

3. Beat granulated sugar, butter and brown sugar in large bowl with electric mixer at medium speed until combined. Add eggs, one at a time, beating until blended after each addition. Add orange juice and orange peel; beat until blended.

4. Whisk flour, baking powder, ginger, cinnamon, salt and allspice in medium bowl. Gradually add to butter mixture, beating until blended after each addition. Stir in fruit and pecans. Spoon batter evenly into prepared muffin cups.

5. Bake 15 minutes or until toothpick inserted into centers comes out clean. Cool in pans 5 minutes; remove to wire racks.

6. Meanwhile, combine powdered sugar and lemon juice in small bowl. Brush glaze on top of cupcakes while still warm; cool completely.

Makes 28 mini cupcakes

Tip: If you don't have mini muffin pans, arrange mini foil baking cups on ungreased cookie sheets. Fill and bake as directed, being careful to get batter into the center of cups so that they do not tip over.

Hot Chocolate Cupcakes

1 package (about 16 ounces) pound cake mix, plus ingredients to prepare mix
4 containers (4 ounces each) prepared chocolate pudding*
2½ cups whipped topping, divided
4 small chewy chocolate candies
Unsweetened cocoa powder (optional)

**Or purchase 1 (4-serving size) package instant chocolate pudding and pie filling mix and prepare according to package directions. Use 2 cups pudding for recipe; reserve remaining pudding for another use.*

1. Preheat oven to 350°F. Spray 15 standard (2½-inch) muffin cups with baking spray (nonstick cooking spray with flour added) or grease and flour cups. Prepare cake mix according to package directions. Spoon batter into prepared muffin cups, filling about two-thirds full.
2. Bake 20 minutes or until toothpick inserted into centers comes out clean. Cool in pans 10 minutes. Remove to wire racks; cool completely.
3. Combine chocolate pudding and 2 cups whipped topping in medium bowl until well blended; refrigerate until ready to use.
4. Working with one at a time, unwrap chocolate candies and microwave on LOW (30%) 5 to 10 seconds or until slightly softened. Stretch into long thin rope; cut ropes into 2-inch lengths. Curve candy pieces into "C" shape to resemble handles of mugs.
5. Cut out 2-inch hole from top of each cupcake with small paring knife. Cut two slits, ½ inch apart, in one side of each cupcake. Insert chocolate candy into slits. Fill top of each cupcake with chocolate pudding mixture. Top with small dollop of remaining whipped topping; sprinkle with cocoa, if desired.

Makes 15 cupcakes

Red Velvet Cupcakes

- 2¼ cups all-purpose flour
- 1 teaspoon salt
- 2 bottles (1 ounce each) red food coloring
- 3 tablespoons unsweetened cocoa powder
- 1 cup buttermilk
- 1 teaspoon vanilla
- 1½ cups sugar
- ½ cup (1 stick) unsalted butter, softened
- 2 eggs
- 1 teaspoon white vinegar
- 1 teaspoon baking soda
- 1 to 2 containers (16 ounces each) whipped cream cheese frosting
- Toasted coconut* (optional)

**To toast coconut, spread evenly on ungreased baking sheet. Bake in preheated 350°F oven 5 to 7 minutes or until light golden brown, stirring occasionally.*

1. Preheat oven to 350°F. Line 18 standard (2½-inch) muffin cups with paper baking cups.
2. Combine flour and salt in medium bowl. Gradually stir food coloring into cocoa in small bowl until blended and smooth. Combine buttermilk and vanilla in another small bowl.
3. Beat sugar and butter in large bowl with electric mixer at medium speed 4 minutes or until light and fluffy. Add eggs, one at a time, beating well after each addition. Add cocoa mixture; beat until well blended and uniform in color. Add flour mixture alternately with buttermilk mixture, beating just until blended. Stir vinegar into baking soda in small bowl; gently fold into batter with spatula or spoon (do not use mixer). Spoon batter into prepared muffin cups, filling two-thirds full.
4. Bake 20 minutes or until toothpick inserted into centers comes out clean. Cool in pans 10 minutes. Remove to wire racks; cool completely.
5. Generously spread frosting over cupcakes. Sprinkle with coconut, if desired.

Makes 18 cupcakes

Sweet Snowflakes

- 1 package (about 18 ounces) white cake mix, plus ingredients to prepare mix
- White frosting
- 4 ounces almond bark or white chocolate candy discs
- Silver, pearl or blue decorating sugar and decors

1. Preheat oven to 350°F. Line 24 standard (2½-inch) muffin cups with paper baking cups. Prepare cake mix according to package directions. Spoon batter into prepared muffin cups, filling two-thirds full. Bake 20 minutes or until toothpick inserted into centers comes out clean. Cool in pans 10 minutes. Remove to wire racks; cool completely. Frost cupcakes.

2. Place large piece of waxed paper on work surface. Melt almond bark according to package directions; place in plastic squeeze bottle or piping bag fitted with small writing tip. Pipe snowflake shapes onto waxed paper, a few at a time. Decorate with sugar and decors as desired. Repeat to create 24 large or 48 small snowflakes. Let stand 15 minutes. Stick snowflakes into frosting.

Makes 24 cupcakes

Holiday Poke Cupcakes

- 1 package (2-layer size) white cake mix
- 1 cup boiling water
- 1 package (4-serving size) JELL-O® Brand Gelatin, any red flavor
- 1 tub (8 ounces) COOL WHIP® Whipped Topping, thawed
- Red or green food coloring
- Suggested decorations: colored sugar, sprinkles, crushed candy canes and/or JET-PUFFED® HOLIDAY MALLOWS Marshmallows

PREPARE batter and bake as directed for cupcakes. Cool in pans 10 minutes. Pierce tops with fork.

STIR boiling water into dry gelatin mix until dissolved; spoon over cupcakes. Refrigerate 30 minutes. Remove from pans.

TINT whipped topping with food coloring; spread over cupcakes. Decorate as desired. Store in refrigerator.

Makes 24 cupcakes

Sweet Snowflakes

Butter Pecan Cupcakes

- 2 cups chopped pecans
- 3 cups all-purpose flour
- 2 teaspoons baking powder
- ½ teaspoon salt
- 2 cups sugar
- 1 cup (2 sticks) unsalted butter, softened
- 4 eggs
- ¾ cup milk
- ¼ cup canola or vegetable oil
- 1½ teaspoons vanilla
- Browned Butter Frosting (recipe follows)
- Toasted whole pecans (optional)

1. Preheat oven to 350°F. Line 30 standard (2½-inch) muffin cups with paper baking cups.
2. Spread chopped pecans in shallow baking pan. Bake 5 minutes or until lightly toasted, stirring occasionally. Transfer to plate; cool completely.
3. Whisk flour, baking powder and salt in medium bowl. Beat sugar and butter in large bowl with electric mixer at medium speed until creamy. Add eggs, one at a time, beating well after each addition.
4. Combine milk, oil and vanilla in small bowl. Alternately add flour mixture and milk mixture to butter mixture, beating well after each addition. Stir in chopped pecans. Spoon batter evenly into prepared muffin cups.
5. Bake 20 minutes or until toothpick inserted into centers comes out clean. Cool in pans 10 minutes. Remove to wire racks; cool completely.
6. Meanwhile, prepare Browned Butter Frosting. Pipe or spread onto cupcakes. Garnish with whole pecans.

Makes 30 cupcakes

Browned Butter Frosting: Melt 1 cup (2 sticks) unsalted butter in small saucepan over medium heat. Cook and stir until light brown. Remove from heat; let stand 10 minutes. Combine browned butter, 5½ cups powdered sugar, ¼ cup milk, 1½ teaspoons vanilla and ⅛ teaspoon salt in large bowl. Beat with electric mixer at medium speed until smooth. Add additional milk, 1 tablespoon at a time, if frosting is too stiff. Makes about 4 cups.

Glazed Cranberry Mini-Cakes

- ⅓ cup butter or margarine, softened
- ⅓ cup granulated sugar
- ⅓ cup packed light brown sugar
- 1 egg
- 1¼ teaspoons vanilla extract
- 1⅓ cups all-purpose flour
- ¾ teaspoon baking powder
- ¼ teaspoon baking soda
- ¼ teaspoon salt
- 2 tablespoons milk
- 1¼ cups coarsely chopped fresh cranberries
- ½ cup coarsely chopped walnuts
- 1⅔ cups HERSHEY'S Premier White Chips, divided
- White Glaze (recipe follows)

1. Heat oven to 350°F. Lightly grease or paper-line 36 small muffin cups (1¾ inches in diameter).

2. Beat butter, granulated sugar, brown sugar, egg and vanilla in large bowl until fluffy. Stir together flour, baking powder, baking soda and salt; gradually blend into butter mixture. Add milk; stir until blended. Stir in cranberries, walnuts and ⅔ cup white chips (reserve remaining chips for glaze). Fill muffin cups almost full with batter.

3. Bake 18 to 20 minutes or until wooden pick inserted in center comes out clean. Cool 5 minutes; remove from pans to wire rack. Cool completely. Prepare White Glaze; drizzle over top of mini-cakes. Refrigerate 10 minutes to set glaze.

Makes about 3 dozen mini-cakes

White Glaze: Place remaining 1 cup HERSHEY'S Premier White Chips in small microwave-safe bowl; sprinkle 2 tablespoons vegetable oil over chips. Microwave at MEDIUM (50%) 30 seconds; stir. If necessary, microwave at MEDIUM an additional 30 seconds or just until chips are melted when stirred.

Festive Chocolate Cupcakes

- ¾ cup all-purpose flour
- ½ cup unsweetened cocoa powder
- 1 teaspoon baking powder
- ½ teaspoon salt
- ½ cup (1 stick) butter, softened
- 1 cup plus 2 tablespoons granulated sugar
- 2 eggs
- 1 teaspoon vanilla
- ½ cup whole milk
- 1½ cups prepared chocolate frosting
- Powdered sugar

1. Preheat oven to 350°F. Line 12 standard (2½-inch) muffin cups with paper baking cups.
2. Whisk flour, cocoa, baking powder and salt in small bowl. Beat butter in large bowl with electric mixer at medium speed until creamy. Add granulated sugar; beat 3 to 4 minutes. Add eggs, one at a time, beating well after each addition. Beat in vanilla. Add flour mixture alternately with milk, beginning and ending with flour mixture. Spoon batter into prepared cups, filling about two-thirds full.
3. Bake 20 minutes or until toothpick inserted into centers comes out clean. Cool in pan 10 minutes. Remove to wire rack; cool completely.
4. Microwave frosting in medium microwavable bowl on MEDIUM (50%) 30 seconds; stir. Microwave at additional 15-second intervals until frosting is melted. (Consistency will be thin.) Dip tops of cupcakes in melted frosting; return to wire rack to allow frosting to set. (Frosting may need to be reheated several times to maintain melted consistency.)
5. When frosting is set, place stencil gently over frosting. Sprinkle powdered sugar over cupcake; carefully remove stencil.

Makes 12 cupcakes

Tip Stencils can be found at craft stores and baking supply stores. You can also make your own stencils by cutting out shapes from heavy paper or cardstock.

Pistachio-Chocolate Chip Cupcakes

- 2 cups all-purpose flour
- 1½ cups sugar
- 4 teaspoons baking powder
- ½ teaspoon salt
- ½ cup (1 stick) unsalted butter, softened
- 1 cup milk
- 1 teaspoon vanilla
- 3 eggs
- 1 cup chopped pistachios, plus additional for garnish
- 1 cup mini semisweet chocolate chips
- 2 containers (15 ounces each) vanilla frosting
- ¾ cup marshmallow creme
- Green gel food coloring

1. Preheat oven to 350°F. Line 24 standard (2½-inch) muffin cups with paper baking cups.

2. Beat flour, sugar, baking powder and salt in large bowl with electric mixer at low speed until blended. Add butter; beat at medium speed 30 seconds. Add milk and vanilla; beat 2 minutes. Add eggs; beat 2 minutes. Stir in pistachios and chocolate chips. Spoon batter evenly into prepared baking cups.

3. Bake 20 minutes or until toothpick inserted into centers comes out clean. Cool in pans 10 minutes. Remove to wire racks; cool completely.

4. Combine frosting, marshmallow creme and food coloring in medium bowl until blended. Pipe or spread onto cupcakes. Sprinkle with additional pistachios.

Makes 24 cupcakes

Peppermint Mocha Cupcakes

- 1 package (about 18 ounces) dark chocolate cake mix, plus ingredients to prepare mix
- 1 tablespoon instant espresso powder
- 1½ cups whipping cream
- 1 package (12 ounces) semisweet chocolate chips
- 2 teaspoons peppermint extract
- Crushed candy canes or peppermint candies

1. Preheat oven to 350°F. Line 24 standard (2½-inch) muffin cups with paper baking cups. Prepare cake mix according to package directions; stir in espresso powder. Bake 20 minutes or until toothpick inserted into centers comes out clean. Cool in pans 10 minutes. Remove to wire racks; cool completely.

2. Bring cream to a simmer in small saucepan over medium heat. Place chocolate chips in medium bowl. Pour hot cream over chocolate chips; let stand 2 minutes. Whisk mixture until smooth. Stir in peppermint extract.

3. Place wire rack over waxed paper. Dip tops of cupcakes into chocolate mixture; place on wire rack. Let stand 10 minutes; repeat, if desired. Sprinkle tops with crushed candy canes.

Makes 24 cupcakes

Lovin' Sweetcakes

- 1 package (2-layer size) white cake mix
- 1 package (4-serving size) JELL-O® Strawberry Flavor Gelatin, or any red flavor
- 1 tub (8 ounces) COOL WHIP® Whipped Topping, thawed
- ¼ cup seasonal colored sprinkles

PREPARE cake batter as directed on package. Stir in dry powdered gelatin until well blended.

LINE 24 medium muffin cups with paper liners. Pour batter evenly into cups, filling each cup ½ full. Bake as directed on package for cupcakes. Cool completely.

SPREAD 2 tablespoons whipped topping onto top of each cupcake. Decorate each with ¼ teaspoon sprinkles as desired. Store cupcakes in refrigerator.

Makes 24 servings

Variation: For heart-shaped cupcakes, place a small marble or ½-inch ball of foil between each liner and one side of the cup, pushing the paper in to form a heart shape. Bake as directed on package for cupcakes. Cool completely; remove marble or foil.

Peppermint Mocha Cupcakes

Chai Latte Cupcakes

- 7 chai tea bags, divided
- 1½ cups boiling water
- 1 package (about 18 ounces) white cake mix
- 3 eggs
- ⅓ cup vegetable oil
- 1 cup milk
- 2 to 3 cups powdered sugar
- Turbinado sugar (optional)

1. Place 4 tea bags in small heatproof bowl. Pour water over top; allow tea bags to steep until cooled slightly. Squeeze tea bags; discard.

2. Preheat oven to 350°F. Line 22 standard (2½-inch) muffin cups with paper baking cups.

3. Combine cake mix, prepared tea, eggs and oil in large bowl with electric mixer at medium speed 2 minutes or until well blended. Spoon batter evenly into prepared muffin cups.

4. Bake 20 minutes or until toothpick inserted into centers comes out clean. Cool in pans 10 minutes. Remove to wire rack; cool completely.

5. Bring milk to a simmer in small saucepan over medium heat; remove from heat. Add remaining 3 tea bags; allow to steep until slightly cooled. Remove and discard tea bags. Whisk in powdered sugar until smooth and thick enough for dipping.

6. Set wire rack over waxed paper. Dip tops of cupcakes into glaze; place on wire rack. Sprinkle with turbinado sugar, if desired. Let stand 10 minutes or until set.

Makes 22 cupcakes

Christmas Tree Cupcakes

- 1 package (about 18 ounces) white cake mix, plus ingredients to prepare mix
- ¼ cup crushed peppermint candies
- Buttercream Frosting (recipe follows)
- 8 dark chocolate sticks
- White icing writing pen
- Mini candy-coated chocolate pieces
- Star-shaped candy decors

1. Preheat oven to 350°F. Arrange 11 triangle-shaped silicone cupcake liners in 13×9-inch baking pan. Fill in empty spaces with crumpled foil to keep liners in place. Spray liners with nonstick cooking spray.

2. Prepare cake mix according to package directions. Fold in crushed candies. Pour half of batter into liners, filling two-thirds full. Bake 20 minutes or until toothpick inserted into centers comes out clean. Cool in pan 5 minutes. Remove to wire rack; cool completely. Remove from liners. Repeat with remaining batter.

3. Prepare Buttercream Frosting; frost cupcakes. Cut each dark chocolate stick into 3 equal pieces. Insert chocolate piece into bottom of each cupcake for tree trunk. Use icing pen to draw on garland. Decorate trees with chocolate pieces. Place candy stars on top of trees.

Makes 22 cupcakes

Buttercream Frosting

- 1½ cups (3 sticks) unsalted butter, softened
- 1 tablespoon vanilla
- ½ teaspoon salt
- 1 tablespoon plus 1½ teaspoons meringue powder
- 1 tablespoon plus 1½ teaspoons milk
- 1½ packages (16 ounces each) powdered sugar
- Green food coloring

1. Beat butter, vanilla and salt in large bowl with electric mixer at medium speed until light and fluffy, scraping side of bowl. Beat in meringue powder and milk.

2. Gradually add powdered sugar, beating until incorporated. Beat at high speed 5 minutes or until light and fluffy. Stir in food coloring. Use immediately or refrigerate up to 1 week. If refrigerated, bring to room temperature and rewhip before using.

Makes 6 cups

Peanut Butter Cupcakes

- 1 cup creamy peanut butter, divided
- ¼ cup (½ stick) unsalted butter, softened
- 1 cup packed light brown sugar
- 2 eggs
- 2 cups all-purpose flour
- 2 teaspoons baking powder
- ½ teaspoon baking soda
- ½ teaspoon salt
- 1 cup milk
- 1½ cups mini semisweet chocolate chips, divided, plus additional for garnish
- Peanut Buttery Frosting (recipe follows)

1. Preheat oven to 350°F. Line 24 standard (2½-inch) muffin cups with paper baking cups.

2. Beat ½ cup peanut butter and butter in large bowl with electric mixer at medium speed until blended. Add brown sugar; beat until well blended. Add eggs, one at a time, beating well after each addition.

3. Whisk flour, baking powder, baking soda and salt in small bowl. Add flour mixture alternately with milk to peanut butter mixture; beat at low speed until well blended. Stir in 1 cup chocolate chips.

4. Spoon batter evenly into prepared muffin cups. Bake 15 minutes or until toothpick inserted into centers comes out clean. (Cover with foil if tops of cupcakes begin to brown too much.) Cool completely in pans on wire racks. Meanwhile, prepare Peanut Buttery Frosting.

5. Pipe or spread cupcakes with Peanut Butter Frosting. Place remaining ½ cup peanut butter in small microwavable bowl. Microwave on HIGH 15 seconds or until melted. Place remaining ½ cup chocolate chips in another small microwavable bowl. Microwave on HIGH 15 seconds or until melted. Drizzle peanut butter and chocolate over frosting. Garnish with additional chocolate chips. *Makes 24 cupcakes*

Peanut Buttery Frosting: Beat ½ cup (1 stick) softened unsalted butter and ½ cup creamy peanut butter in medium bowl with electric mixer at medium speed until smooth. Gradually add 2 cups sifted powdered sugar and ½ teaspoon vanilla until blended. Add 3 to 6 tablespoons milk, 1 tablespoon at a time, until smooth. Makes about 3 cups.

Chocolate Overload

Dark Chocolate Banana Cupcakes

- 1½ cups all-purpose flour
- 1½ cups granulated sugar
- ½ cup unsweetened Dutch-process cocoa powder
- 2 tablespoons packed brown sugar
- 2 teaspoons baking powder
- ½ teaspoon salt
- ½ cup vegetable oil
- 2 eggs
- ¼ cup buttermilk
- 1 teaspoon vanilla
- 2 mashed bananas (about 1 cup)
- 1½ cups whipping cream
- 2 cups dark chocolate chips
- Dried banana chips (optional)

1. Preheat oven to 350°F. Line 18 standard (2½-inch) muffin cups with paper baking cups.

2. Whisk flour, granulated sugar, cocoa, brown sugar, baking powder and salt in large bowl. Add oil, eggs, milk and vanilla; beat with electric mixer at medium speed 2 minutes or until well blended. Beat in bananas until well blended. Spoon batter into prepared muffin cups, filling three-fourths full.

3. Bake 25 minutes or until toothpick inserted into centers comes out clean. Cool in pans 10 minutes. Remove to wire racks; cool completely.

4. Bring cream to a simmer in small saucepan over medium heat. Place chocolate chips in medium bowl. Pour hot cream over chocolate chips; let stand 2 minutes. Whisk mixture until smooth.

5. Place wire rack over waxed paper. Dip tops of cupcakes into chocolate mixture; place on wire rack. Let stand 10 minutes; dip again, if desired. Drizzle banana chips with chocolate mixture and place on top of cupcakes, if desired. *Makes 18 cupcakes*

Iced Coffee Cupcakes

1 package (about 18 ounces) chocolate fudge cake mix *without* pudding in the mix
1 package (4-serving size) instant chocolate pudding and pie filling mix
1⅓ cups brewed coffee, cooled to room temperature
3 eggs
½ cup vegetable oil
1 teaspoon vanilla
½ gallon mocha almond fudge or coffee ice cream, softened
1 bottle (7¼ ounces) quick-hardening chocolate shell dessert topping
½ cup pecan pieces, toasted*

**To toast pecans, spread in single layer on baking sheet. Bake in preheated 350°F oven 5 to 7 minutes or until fragrant, stirring frequently.*

1. Preheat oven to 350°F. Line 20 standard (2½-inch) muffin cups with foil or paper baking cups or spray with nonstick cooking spray.

2. Beat cake mix, pudding mix, coffee, eggs, oil and vanilla in large bowl with electric mixer at low speed 30 seconds. Beat at medium speed 2 minutes or until well blended. Spoon batter into prepared muffin cups, filling three-fourths full.

3. Bake 20 minutes or until toothpick inserted into centers comes out clean. Cool in pans 10 minutes. Remove to wire racks; cool completely.

4. Remove 1 tablespoon cake from center of one cupcake. Fill with 2 to 3 tablespoons ice cream, mounding slightly. Spoon about 1 tablespoon chocolate shell topping over ice cream; quickly sprinkle with pecans before topping hardens. Place cupcake in freezer until ready to serve. Repeat with remaining cupcakes, ice cream, topping and pecans.

Makes 20 cupcakes

Truffle Brownie Bites

Brownies

- ⅔ cup semisweet chocolate chips
- ½ cup (1 stick) unsalted butter, cut into chunks
- 1⅓ cups sugar
- 3 eggs
- 1 teaspoon vanilla
- 1 cup minus 2 tablespoons all-purpose flour
- ½ teaspoon salt

Ganache

- 7 tablespoons whipping cream
- ¾ cup semisweet chocolate chips
- Colored sprinkles

1. Preheat oven to 350°F. Line 36 mini (1¾-inch) muffin cups with foil or paper baking cups.

2. For brownies, combine ⅔ cup chocolate chips and butter in large microwavable bowl. Microwave on HIGH 30 seconds; stir. Repeat as necessary until chips are melted and mixture is smooth. Let cool slightly.

3. Add sugar to melted chocolate mixture; beat until well blended. Add eggs, one at a time, beating after each addition. Stir in vanilla. Add flour and salt; beat until well blended. Spoon batter into prepared muffin cups, filling about three-fourths full.

4. Bake 15 minutes or until tops are firm to the touch. Cool in pans 5 minutes. Remove to wire racks; cool completely.

5. For ganache, bring cream to a simmer in small saucepan over medium heat. Remove from heat; add ¾ cup chocolate chips. Stir until chips are melted and mixture is smooth. Let stand 2 minutes to thicken and cool slightly.

6. Dip tops of brownies into ganache; smooth surface. Decorate with sprinkles. Refrigerate 30 minutes or until ganache is set. Store in refrigerator.

Makes 36 brownies

Mini Oreo® Surprise Cupcakes

- 1 package (2-layer size) chocolate cake mix
- 1 package (8 ounces) PHILADELPHIA® Cream Cheese, softened
- 1 egg
- 2 tablespoons sugar
- 48 Mini OREO® Bite Size Chocolate Sandwich Cookies
- 1½ cups thawed COOL WHIP® Whipped Topping

PREHEAT oven to 350°F. Prepare cake batter as directed on package; set aside. Beat cream cheese, egg and sugar until well blended.

SPOON cake batter into 24 paper- or foil-lined 2½-inch muffin cups, filling each cup about half full. Top each with about 1½ teaspoons of the cream cheese mixture and 1 cookie. Cover evenly with remaining cake batter.

BAKE 19 to 22 minutes or until wooden toothpick inserted in centers comes out clean. Cool 5 minutes; remove from pans to wire racks. Cool completely. (There may be an indentation in top of each cupcake after baking.) Top cupcakes with whipped topping and remaining cookies just before serving. Store in tightly covered container in refrigerator up to 3 days.

Makes 24 cupcakes

Prep Time: 10 minutes
Bake Time: 22 minutes

For easy portioning of cream cheese mixture into cake batter, spoon cream cheese mixture into large resealable plastic bag. Seal bag securely. Snip small corner of bag with scissors. Squeeze about 1½ teaspoons of the cream cheese mixture over batter in each muffin cup.

Chocolate Hazelnut Cupcakes

1¾ cups all-purpose flour
1½ teaspoons baking powder
½ teaspoon salt
2 cups chocolate hazelnut spread, divided
⅓ cup (⅔ stick) butter, softened
¾ cup sugar
2 eggs
1 teaspoon vanilla
1¼ cups milk
Chopped hazelnuts (optional)

1. Preheat oven to 350°F. Line 18 standard (2½-inch) muffin cups with paper or foil baking cups.

2. Whisk flour, baking powder and salt in medium bowl. Beat ⅓ cup chocolate hazelnut spread and butter in large bowl with electric mixer at medium speed until smooth. Beat in sugar until well blended. Beat in eggs and vanilla. Add flour mixture alternately with milk, beginning and ending with flour mixture, beating until blended. Spoon batter into prepared muffin cups, filling two-thirds full.

3. Bake 20 minutes or until toothpick inserted into centers comes out clean. Cool in pans 10 minutes. Remove to wire racks; cool completely.

4. Frost cupcakes with remaining 1⅔ cups chocolate hazelnut spread. Sprinkle with hazelnuts.

Makes 18 cupcakes

Quick Cookie Cupcakes

1 package (about 16 ounces) refrigerated break-apart chocolate chip cookie dough (24 count)
1½ cups prepared chocolate frosting
Colored decors

1. Preheat oven to 350°F. Line 24 mini (1¾-inch) muffin cups with paper baking cups.

2. Break dough into 24 pieces along score lines. Roll each piece into a ball; place in prepared muffin cups. Bake 10 to 12 minutes or until golden brown. Cool in pans 5 minutes. Remove to wire racks; cool completely.

3. Pipe or spread frosting over each cupcake. Sprinkle with decors.

Makes 24 mini cupcakes

Chocolate Hazelnut Cupcakes

Chocolate Moose

1 package (about 18 ounces) chocolate cake mix, plus ingredients to prepare mix
1 container (16 ounces) milk chocolate frosting
½ to ¾ cup vanilla frosting
1 package (12 ounces) semisweet chocolate chips
2 tablespoons shortening
White round candies
Small black candies
Black decorating gel
Pretzel twists

1. Preheat oven to 350°F. Line 22 standard (2½-inch) muffin cups with paper baking cups.

2. Prepare cake mix according to package directions. Spoon batter into prepared muffin cups, filling two-thirds full. Bake 20 minutes or until toothpick inserted into centers comes out clean. Cool in pans 10 minutes. Remove to wire racks; cool completely.

3. Combine chocolate frosting and ½ cup vanilla frosting in medium bowl until well blended. Frost cupcakes.

4. Place chocolate chips and shortening in medium microwavable bowl. Microwave on HIGH 1½ minutes or until chocolate is melted and mixture is smooth, stirring every 30 seconds. Place chocolate in pastry bag or small food storage bag with small corner cut off. Pipe chocolate mixture into shape of moose head on each cupcake as shown in photo; smooth chocolate with small spatula. (Chocolate may need to be reheated slightly if it becomes too stiff to pipe.)

5. Arrange candies on cupcakes to create eyes and noses. Pipe small dot of decorating gel or chocolate mixture onto each white candy for eyes. Break off small section of each pretzel twist to form antlers. Push ends of pretzels into top of cupcakes.

Makes 22 cupcakes

Midnight Chocolate Cheesecake Cookie Cups

¼ cup (½ stick) butter, softened
¼ cup shortening
½ cup sugar
1 egg
½ teaspoon vanilla extract
1 cup all-purpose flour
2 tablespoons HERSHEY'S SPECIAL DARK® Cocoa or HERSHEY'S Cocoa
½ teaspoon baking powder
⅛ teaspoon salt
Chocolate Filling (recipe follows)
Whipped topping or sweetened whipped cream
30 HERSHEY'S KISSES® BRAND SPECIAL DARK® Mildly Sweet Chocolates, unwrapped

1. Heat oven to 350°F. Paper or foil line 30 small (1¾-inch diameter) muffin cups.

2. Beat butter and shortening in medium bowl until fluffy. Beat in sugar, egg and vanilla. Stir together flour, cocoa, baking powder and salt. Gradually blend into butter mixture, blending well.

3. Drop rounded teaspoonful of dough into each prepared muffin cup. Using back of spoon, push dough up sides of muffin cup forming crater in cup. (If you have difficulty with this step, refrigerate pans for about 10 minutes and then continue.) Prepare Chocolate Filling; evenly divide into muffin cups. (Cups will be very full.)

4. Bake 15 minutes or until cheesecake is set. Cool completely in pan on wire rack. Cover; refrigerate until ready to serve. To serve, top each cheesecake with whipped topping rosette and chocolate piece.

Makes 30 dessert cups

Chocolate Filling: Beat 2 packages (3 ounces each) softened cream cheese and ¼ cup sugar until well blended. Beat in 1 egg, 1 teaspoon vanilla extract and ⅛ teaspoon salt. Place 12 unwrapped HERSHEY'S KISSES® BRAND SPECIAL DARK® Mildly Sweet Chocolates in small microwave-safe bowl. Microwave at MEDIUM (50%) 15 seconds at a time, stirring after each heating, until chocolates are melted and smooth when stirred. Cool slightly, blend into cheesecake batter.

White Chocolate Macadamia Cupcakes

- 1 package (about 18 ounces) white cake mix *without* pudding in the mix, plus ingredients to prepare mix
- 1 package (4-serving size) white chocolate instant pudding and pie filling mix
- ¾ cup chopped macadamia nuts
- 1½ cups flaked coconut
- 1 cup white chocolate chips
- 1 container (16 ounces) white frosting

1. Preheat oven to 350°F. Line 22 standard (2½-inch) muffin cups with paper baking cups.
2. Prepare cake mix according to package directions; stir in pudding mix. Fold in nuts. Spoon batter into prepared muffin cups, filling two-thirds full.
3. Bake 20 minutes or until toothpick inserted into centers comes out clean. Cool in pans 10 minutes. Remove to wire racks; cool completely.
4. Meanwhile, spread coconut evenly on ungreased baking sheet; bake 6 minutes or until light golden brown, stirring occasionally. Cool completely.
5. Microwave white chocolate chips in small microwavable bowl on MEDIUM (50%) 2 minutes or until melted and smooth, stirring every 30 seconds. Cool slightly; stir into frosting. Frost cupcakes; sprinkle with toasted coconut.

Makes 22 cupcakes

Coffee Brownie Bites

- 1 package (21 ounces) fudge brownie mix
- 3 eggs
- ½ cup vegetable oil
- 2 teaspoons instant coffee granules
- 2 teaspoons coffee liqueur (optional)
- Powdered sugar (optional)

1. Preheat oven 325°F. Lightly spray 60 mini (1¾-inch) muffin cups with nonstick cooking spray.
2. Combine brownie mix, eggs, oil, coffee granules and coffee liqueur, if desired, in medium bowl. Stir until well blended.
3. Fill each cup with 1 tablespoon brownie mixture. Bake 13 minutes or until toothpick inserted into centers comes out almost clean. Remove to wire rack; cool completely. Sprinkle with powdered sugar, if desired. Store in airtight container.

Makes 60 brownies

Chocolate Caramel Bites

- 1 cup sugar
- ¾ cup plus 2 tablespoons all-purpose flour
- ½ cup unsweetened cocoa powder
- ¾ teaspoon baking soda
- ¾ teaspoon baking powder
- ½ teaspoon salt
- ½ cup plus 2 tablespoons whole milk, divided
- ¼ cup vegetable oil
- 1 egg
- ½ cup boiling water
- 24 caramels (about 7 ounces)
- 1 cup semisweet chocolate chips
- Colored decors (optional)

1. Preheat oven to 350°F. Line 36 mini (1¾-inch) muffin cups with paper baking cups.

2. Whisk sugar, flour, cocoa, baking soda, baking powder and salt in medium bowl. Beat ½ cup milk, oil and egg in large bowl with electric mixer at medium speed until well blended. Add sugar mixture; beat 2 minutes. Add water; beat at low speed until blended. (Batter will be thin.) Pour into prepared muffin cups, filling three-fourths full.

3. Bake 8 minutes. Meanwhile, combine caramels and remaining 2 tablespoons milk in medium microwavable bowl. Microwave on HIGH 1½ minutes; stir. Microwave 1 minute or until caramels are completely melted.

4. Spoon ½ teaspoon caramel sauce over each partially-baked cupcake. Bake 4 minutes or until toothpick inserted near edges of cups comes out clean. Cool in pans 10 minutes. Remove to wire racks; cool completely.

5. Place chocolate chips in small microwavable bowl. Microwave on HIGH 1 minute; stir. Microwave at additional 15-second intervals until chocolate is melted. Reheat remaining caramel sauce in microwave until melted; drizzle chocolate and caramel sauce over cupcakes. Top with decors, if desired.

Makes 36 mini cupcakes

Rocky Road Cupcakes

- 1 package (about 18 ounces) chocolate fudge cake mix
- 1⅓ cups water
- 3 eggs
- ½ cup vegetable oil
- ¾ cup mini semisweet chocolate chips, divided
- 1 container (16 ounces) chocolate frosting
- 1 cup mini marshmallows
- ⅔ cup walnut pieces
- Hot fudge ice cream topping or chocolate syrup, heated

1. Preheat oven to 325°F. Line 22 standard (2½-inch) muffin cups with paper baking cups.

2. Beat cake mix, water, eggs, oil and ¼ cup chocolate chips in large bowl with electric mixer at low speed 30 seconds. Beat at medium speed 2 minutes or until well blended. Spoon batter into prepared muffin cups, filling two-thirds full.

3. Bake 20 minutes or until toothpick inserted into centers comes out clean. Cool in pans 10 minutes. Remove to wire racks; cool completely.

4. Spread thin layer of frosting over cupcakes. Top with marshmallows, walnuts and remaining ½ cup chocolate chips, pressing down lightly to adhere to frosting. Drizzle with hot fudge topping.

Makes 22 cupcakes

Cream Cheese Surprise Cupcakes

- 24 REYNOLDS® Baking Cups
- 1 package (about 18 ounces) chocolate cake mix
- 1 package (8 ounces) cream cheese, softened
- 1 egg, lightly beaten
- ⅓ cup sugar
- 1 cup mini chocolate chips
- 1 container (16 ounces) ready-to-spread cream cheese frosting

Preheat oven to 350°F. Place Reynolds Baking Cups in muffin pans; set aside. Prepare cake mix following package directions for 24 cupcakes. Spoon cake batter into baking cups.

Beat cream cheese, egg and sugar in a bowl, with an electric mixer. Stir in chocolate chips. Drop by heaping tablespoonfuls into cupcake batter.

Bake 18 to 20 minutes or until toothpick inserted in center comes out clean; cool. Frost cupcakes with cream cheese frosting.

Makes 24 servings

Prep Time: 15 minutes
Cook Time: 18 to 20 minutes

Rocky Road Cupcakes

Classic Chocolate Cupcakes

- 1¾ cups all-purpose flour
- 1¼ cups sugar
- 2 teaspoons baking powder
- ½ teaspoon salt
- ¾ cup vegetable oil
- ¾ cup milk
- 3 eggs
- 1½ teaspoons vanilla
- 8 squares (1 ounce each) semisweet baking chocolate, melted and cooled slightly
- Chocolate Buttercream Frosting (recipe follows)
- Colored sprinkles (optional)

1. Preheat oven to 350°F. Line 20 standard (2½-inch) muffin cups with paper baking cups.

2. Whisk flour, sugar, baking powder and salt in large bowl. Add oil, milk, eggs and vanilla; beat with electric mixer at medium speed 2 minutes or until well blended. Stir in melted chocolate until well blended. Spoon batter into prepared muffin cups, filling three-fourths full.

3. Bake 25 minutes or until toothpick inserted into centers comes out clean. Cool in pans 10 minutes. Remove to wire racks; cool completely.

4. Prepare Chocolate Buttercream Frosting; pipe or spread onto cupcakes. Decorate with sprinkles, if desired.

Makes 20 cupcakes

Chocolate Buttercream Frosting

- 4 cups powdered sugar, sifted, divided
- ¾ cup butter, softened
- 6 squares (1 ounce each) unsweetened chocolate, melted
- 6 to 8 tablespoons milk, divided
- ¾ teaspoon vanilla

1. Combine 2 cups powdered sugar, butter, melted chocolate, 4 tablespoons milk and vanilla in large bowl. Beat with electric mixer at medium speed until smooth.

2. Add remaining 2 cups sugar; beat until light and fluffy, adding more milk, 1 tablespoon at a time, if needed to reach desired spreading consistency.

Makes about 3 cups

Triple Chocolate PB Minis

- 2 packages (4.4 ounces each) chocolate peanut butter cups
- 1 package (about 18 ounces) chocolate fudge cake mix, plus ingredients to prepare mix
- ¾ cup whipping cream
- 1½ cups semisweet chocolate chips

1. Preheat oven to 350°F. Line 60 mini (1¾-inch) muffin cups with paper baking cups. Finely chop peanut butter cups; refrigerate while preparing batter.
2. Prepare cake mix according to package directions; stir in 1 cup chopped peanut butter cups. Spoon batter into prepared muffin cups, filling two-thirds full.
3. Bake 10 minutes or until toothpick inserted into centers comes out clean. Cool in pans 5 minutes. Remove to wire racks; cool completely.
4. Meanwhile, bring cream to a simmer in small saucepan over medium heat. Place chocolate chips in small heatproof bowl; pour cream over chips. Let stand 5 minutes; stir until blended and smooth. Glaze will thicken as it cools (or refrigerate glaze to thicken more quickly).
5. Dip tops of cupcakes in chocolate glaze; sprinkle with remaining chopped candy.

Makes 60 mini cupcakes

Tip

Chopping chocolate or candies can be difficult. If the room is warm or you handle the chocolate too much, it can become soft. When you try to chop it, you'll end up with a paste rather than pieces. Refrigerating the peanut butter cups for 15 or 20 minutes before chopping will make the process much easier.

Monkey A-Rounds

- 1 package (about 18 ounces) chocolate cake mix, plus ingredients to prepare mix
- 1 container (16 ounces) chocolate frosting
- 1 container (16 ounces) white frosting
- Yellow food coloring
- 44 chocolate discs
- Small black jelly beans
- Black string licorice

1. Preheat oven to 350°F. Line 22 standard (2½-inch) muffin cups with paper baking cups. Prepare cake mix according to package directions. Spoon batter into prepared muffin cups, filling two-thirds full.

2. Bake 20 minutes or until toothpick inserted into centers comes out clean. Cool in pans 10 minutes. Remove to wire racks; cool completely.

3. Frost cupcakes with chocolate frosting. Place white frosting in small bowl. Add food coloring, a few drops at a time, until desired shade of yellow is reached. Transfer frosting to pastry bag or small food storage bag with small corner cut off.

4. Pipe circle of yellow frosting in center of each chocolate disc for ears. Cut jelly beans in half crosswise for eyes; cut licorice into smaller lengths for mouths and noses. Pipe yellow frosting into oval shape on each cupcake as shown in photo; arrange eyes just above oval and ears on either side of cupcake. Arrange licorice noses and mouths inside oval. Use toothpick or knife to pull up frosting at top of cupcake into hair (or use pastry bag with special tip to pipe hair).

Makes 22 cupcakes

Chocolate Chip Cookie Cupcakes

- 1 package (about 18 ounces) yellow cake mix, plus ingredients to prepare mix
- 1½ cups semisweet chocolate chips, divided
- 1½ cups chopped walnuts or pecans, divided
- 1 container (16 ounces) cream cheese frosting
- ¾ cup creamy peanut butter

1. Preheat oven to 350°F. Line 24 standard (2½-inch) muffin cups with paper baking cups.

2. Prepare cake mix according to package directions; stir in ¾ cup chocolate chips and ¾ cup walnuts. Spoon batter into prepared muffin cups, filling two-thirds full.

3. Bake 20 minutes or until toothpick inserted into centers comes out clean. Cool in pans 10 minutes. Remove to wire racks; cool completely.

4. Combine frosting and peanut butter in medium bowl until well blended. Frost cupcakes; sprinkle with remaining ¾ cup chocolate chips and ¾ cup walnuts. *Makes 24 cupcakes*

Molten Cinnamon-Chocolate Cakes

- 6 ounces semisweet chocolate
- ¾ cup (1½ sticks) butter
- 1½ cups powdered sugar
- 4 eggs
- 6 tablespoons all-purpose flour
- 1½ teaspoons vanilla
- ¾ teaspoon ground cinnamon
- Powdered sugar

1. Preheat oven to 425°F. Spray 6 jumbo muffin cups or 6 (1-cup) custard cups with nonstick cooking spray.

2. Combine chocolate and butter in medium microwavable bowl; microwave on HIGH 1½ minutes, stirring every 30 seconds, until melted and smooth. Whisk in powdered sugar, eggs, flour, vanilla and cinnamon until well blended. Pour batter into prepared muffin cups, filling two-thirds full.

3. Bake 13 minutes or until cupcakes spring back when lightly touched but centers are soft. Let stand 1 minute; loosen sides with knife. Gently lift out cakes and invert onto serving plates; sprinkle with powdered sugar. Serve immediately. *Makes 6 cakes*

Chocolate Chip Cookie Cupcakes

Mini Brownie Cups

- ¼ cup (½ stick) light margarine
- 2 egg whites
- 1 egg
- ¾ cup sugar
- ⅔ cup all-purpose flour
- ⅓ cup HERSHEY®'S Cocoa
- ½ teaspoon baking powder
- ¼ teaspoon salt
- Mocha Glaze (recipe follows)

1. Heat oven to 350°F. Line small muffin cups (1¾ inches in diameter) with paper bake cups or spray with vegetable cooking spray.

2. Melt margarine in small saucepan over low heat; cool slightly. Beat egg whites and egg in small bowl with electric mixer on medium speed until foamy; gradually add sugar, beating until slightly thickened and light in color. Stir together flour, cocoa, baking powder and salt; gradually add to egg mixture, beating until blended. Gradually add melted margarine, beating just until blended. Fill muffin cups ⅔ full with batter.

3. Bake 15 to 18 minutes or until wooden pick inserted in center comes out clean. Remove from pan to wire rack. Cool completely. Prepare Mocha Glaze; drizzle over tops of brownie cups. Let stand until glaze is set.

Makes 24 servings

Mocha Glaze

- ¼ cup powdered sugar
- ¾ teaspoon HERSHEY®'S Cocoa
- ¼ teaspoon powdered instant coffee
- 2 teaspoons hot water
- ¼ teaspoon vanilla extract

Stir together powdered sugar and cocoa in small bowl. Dissolve instant coffee in water; gradually add to sugar mixture, stirring until well blended. Stir in vanilla.

German Chocolate Cupcakes

- 1 package (about 18 ounces) German chocolate cake mix, plus ingredients to prepare mix
- 1 can (12 ounces) evaporated milk
- ½ cup (1 stick) butter, softened
- 4 egg yolks, beaten
- ¾ cup granulated sugar
- ¼ cup brown sugar
- 2 cups shredded coconut
- 1 cup chopped pecans
- 3 ounces semisweet chocolate, finely chopped

1. Preheat oven to 350°F. Line 22 standard (2½-inch) muffin cups with paper baking cups.

2. Prepare cake mix according to package directions. Spoon batter into prepared muffin cups, filling two-thirds full. Bake 20 minutes or until toothpick inserted into centers comes out clean. Cool in pans 10 minutes. Remove to wire racks; cool completely.

3. Combine evaporated milk, butter, egg yolks, granulated sugar, and brown sugar in medium saucepan. Cook over medium-low heat, stirring constantly, 8 to 10 minutes or until slightly thickened and just beginning to bubble. Stir in coconut and pecans. Remove from heat; let stand about 1 hour or until thickened, stirring occasionally. Spoon cooled coconut mixture evenly over each cupcake.

4. Place chocolate in small microwavable bowl; microwave on HIGH 30 seconds; stir. Microwave at additional 15-second intervals until chocolate is melted. Drizzle chocolate over cupcakes.

Makes 22 cupcakes

Tip

German Chocolate Cake, the inspiration for these cupcakes, has been popular in the United States since the late 1950s but its origins have very little to do with the country of Germany. The original recipe that started the craze over this decadent sweet treat called for a specific type of store-bought baking chocolate which was named after the man who developed it, Sam German.

Filled Rich Chocolate Cupcakes

- Filling (recipe follows)
- 3 cups all-purpose flour
- 2 cups sugar
- ⅔ cup HERSHEY'S Cocoa
- 2 teaspoons baking soda
- 1 teaspoon salt
- 2 cups water
- ⅔ cup vegetable oil
- 2 tablespoons white vinegar
- 2 teaspoons vanilla extract

1. Prepare Filling; set aside. Heat oven to 350°F. Line muffin cups (2½ inches in diameter) with paper bake cups.

2. Stir together flour, sugar, cocoa, baking soda and salt in large bowl. Add water, oil, vinegar and vanilla; beat on medium speed of mixer 3 minutes. Fill muffin cups ⅔ full with batter. Spoon 1 level tablespoon Filling into center of each cupcake.

3. Bake 20 to 25 minutes or until wooden pick inserted in cake portion comes out clean. Remove to wire rack. Cool completely.

Makes about 2½ dozen cupcakes

Filling

- 1 package (8 ounces) cream cheese, softened
- ⅓ cup sugar
- 1 egg
- ⅛ teaspoon salt
- 1 cup HERSHEY'S SPECIAL DARK® Chocolate Chips, HERSHEY'S Semi-Sweet Chocolate Chips or HERSHEY'S Mini Chips Semi-Sweet Chocolate

Beat cream cheese, sugar, egg and salt in small bowl; beat until smooth and creamy. Stir in chocolate chips.

Goblin's Delight Filling: Add 2 teaspoons grated orange peel, 4 drops yellow food color and 3 drops red food color to Filling before stirring in chips.

Valentine Filling: Stir 4 to 5 drops red food color into Filling.

Chocolate Tiramisu Cupcakes

Cupcakes

- 1 package (about 18 ounces) chocolate cake mix
- 1¼ cups water
- 3 eggs
- ⅓ cup melted butter or vegetable oil
- 2 tablespoons instant espresso powder
- 2 tablespoons brandy (optional)

Frosting

- 1 package (8 ounces) cream cheese or mascarpone cheese, softened
- 1½ to 1¾ cups powdered sugar
- 2 tablespoons coffee-flavored liqueur (optional)
- 1 tablespoon unsweetened cocoa powder

1. Preheat oven to 350°F. Line 24 standard (2½-inch) muffin cups with paper baking cups.
2. For cupcakes, beat cake mix, water, eggs, butter, espresso powder and brandy in large bowl with electric mixer at low speed 30 seconds. Beat at medium speed 2 minutes. Spoon batter into prepared muffin cups, filling two-thirds full.
3. Bake 20 minutes or until toothpick inserted into centers comes out clean. Cool in pans 10 minutes. Remove to wire racks; cool completely.
4. For frosting, combine cream cheese and 1½ cups powdered sugar in large bowl; beat at medium speed until well blended. Add liqueur; beat until well blended. If frosting is too soft, beat in additional powdered sugar or chill until desired spreading consistency is reached.
5. Frost cupcakes. Place cocoa in strainer; sprinkle over cupcakes. Store at room temperature up to 24 hours or cover and refrigerate up to 3 days.

Makes 24 cupcakes

Petit Mocha Cheesecakes

- Crumb Crust (recipe follows)
- 1 package (8 ounces) cream cheese, softened
- 1 cup sugar
- 2 eggs
- 1 teaspoon vanilla extract
- ⅓ cup HERSHEY'S Cocoa
- 2 tablespoons all-purpose flour
- 1 tablespoon powdered instant coffee
- 1 teaspoon hot water
- Chocolate Glaze (recipe follows, optional)

1. Heat oven to 375°F. Line small muffin cups (1¾ inches in diameter) with paper baking cups.

2. Prepare Crumb Crust. Place 1 slightly heaping teaspoon crumb mixture into each cup; press lightly. Beat cream cheese in large bowl until fluffy. Add sugar, eggs and vanilla; beat well. Add cocoa and flour; beat well. Dissolve coffee in water; add to chocolate mixture. Place about 1 tablespoon chocolate mixture into each cup.

3. Bake 15 to 18 minutes or until just set. Cool completely in pan on wire rack. Drizzle with Chocolate Glaze, if desired. Refrigerate until cold, about 2 hours. Cover; refrigerate leftover cheesecakes. *Makes 42 cheesecakes*

Crumb Crust: Stir together ½ cup graham cracker crumbs, 2 tablespoons powdered sugar and 2 tablespoons melted butter or margarine in small bowl until well combined.

Chocolate Glaze: Combine ¼ cup HERSHEY'S SPECIAL DARK Chocolate Chips or HERSHEY'S Semi-Sweet Chocolate Chips and 2 tablespoons whipping cream in small saucepan. Cook over very low heat, stirring constantly, until smooth. Use immediately.

Just for Giggles

Grape Soda Cupcakes

1½ cups all-purpose flour
1 (0.14-ounce) envelope grape unsweetened drink mix
2 teaspoons baking powder
⅛ teaspoon salt
1 cup granulated sugar
1 cup (2 sticks) unsalted butter, softened, divided
2 eggs
½ cup plus 3 tablespoons milk, divided
1½ teaspoons vanilla, divided
3 cups powdered sugar
Purple gel food coloring
Pearl decors (optional)

1. Preheat oven to 350°F. Line 12 standard (2½-inch) muffin cups with paper baking cups.

2. Whisk flour, drink mix, baking powder and salt in small bowl. Beat granulated sugar and ½ cup butter in medium bowl with electric mixer at medium speed until creamy. Add eggs, one at a time, beating well after each addition. Add flour mixture; beat until blended. Add ½ cup milk and 1 teaspoon vanilla; beat until smooth.

3. Divide batter evenly into prepared muffin cups. Bake 20 minutes or until toothpick inserted into centers comes out clean. Cool in pan 10 minutes. Remove to wire rack; cool completely.

4. Meanwhile, beat powdered sugar, remaining ½ cup butter, 3 tablespoons milk and ½ teaspoon vanilla in large bowl at medium speed until fluffy. Tint with food coloring. Pipe or spread onto cupcakes. Top with decors, if desired.

Makes 12 cupcakes

Panda Cupcakes

- 1 package (about 18 ounces) yellow cake mix, plus ingredients to prepare mix
- 1 container (16 ounces) vanilla frosting
- 44 large chocolate nonpareil candies or chocolate discs*
- 44 small chocolate nonpareil candies
- 8 ounces semisweet chocolate, chopped *or* 1½ cups semisweet chocolate chips
- 44 white candy sprinkles
- 22 red jelly beans

**Chocolate discs are available at many gourmet, craft and baking supply stores. Large chocolate nonpareil candies may be substituted.*

1. Preheat oven to 350°F. Line 22 standard (2½-inch) muffin cups with paper baking cups. Prepare cake mix according to package directions. Spoon batter into prepared muffin cups, filling two-thirds full.

2. Bake 20 minutes or until toothpick inserted into centers comes out clean. Cool in pans 10 minutes. Remove to wire racks; cool completely.

3. Frost cupcakes. Arrange two chocolate discs on edge of each cupcake for ears. Attach one nonpareil candy to each ear with frosting.

4. Place semisweet chocolate in small food storage bag. Microwave on HIGH about 1½ minutes or until chocolate is melted, kneading bag every 30 seconds. Cut very small hole in corner of bag; pipe kidney shapes for eyes. Place candy sprinkle on each eye. Place jelly bean between eyes for nose. Pipe mouth with melted chocolate. *Makes 22 cupcakes*

Leopard Spots

- 1 package (about 18 ounces) dark chocolate cake mix, plus ingredients to prepare mix
- 3 cups powdered sugar, sifted
- ½ cup (1 stick) unsalted butter, softened
- 3 to 4 tablespoons milk, divided
- ½ teaspoon vanilla
- Brown and yellow gel food coloring
- Black and orange decorating gels

1. Preheat oven to 350°F. Line 24 standard (2½-inch) muffin cups with paper baking cups. Prepare cake mix according to package directions. Spoon batter into prepared muffin cups, filling two-thirds full. Bake 20 minutes or until toothpick inserted into centers comes out clean. Cool in pans 10 minutes. Remove to wire racks; cool completely.

2. Beat powdered sugar, butter, 2 tablespoons milk and vanilla in large bowl with electric mixer at low speed until blended. Beat at high speed until light and fluffy, adding additional milk, 1 teaspoon at a time, to reach spreading consistency. Tint frosting with food coloring to make sandy color. Frost cupcakes.

3. Pipe spots all over tops of cupcakes using black gel to outline and orange gel in centers. *Makes 24 cupcakes*

Pupcakes

- 1 package (about 18 ounces) chocolate cake mix, plus ingredients to prepare mix
- ½ cup (1 stick) butter, softened
- 4 cups powdered sugar
- ¼ to ½ cup half-and-half
- Red and yellow chewy fruit roll-ups
- Candy-coated chocolate pieces
- Assorted colored jelly beans

1. Preheat oven to 350°F. Line 24 standard (2½-inch) muffin cups with paper baking cups. Prepare cake mix according to package directions. Spoon batter into prepared muffin cups, filling two-thirds full. Bake 20 minutes or until toothpick inserted into centers comes out clean. Cool in pans 10 minutes. Remove to wire racks; cool completely.

2. Beat butter in large bowl with electric mixer until creamy. Beat in powdered sugar. Gradually add half-and-half, beating until frosting reaches desired consistency. Frost cupcakes.

3. Cut out ear and tongue shapes from fruit roll-ups with scissors; press into frosting. Add chocolate pieces and jelly beans to create eyes and noses. *Makes 24 cupcakes*

Leopard Spots

Cream-Filled Cupcakes

- 1 package (about 18 ounces) dark chocolate cake mix, plus ingredients to prepare mix
- ½ cup (1 stick) unsalted butter, softened
- ¼ cup shortening
- 3 cups powdered sugar
- 1⅓ cups whipping cream, divided
- 1 teaspoon salt
- 2 cups semisweet chocolate chips

1. Preheat oven to 350°F. Line 24 standard (2½-inch) muffin cups with paper baking cups. Prepare cake mix according to package directions. Spoon batter into prepared muffin cups, filling two-thirds full.

2. Bake 20 minutes or until toothpick inserted into centers comes out clean. Cool in pans 10 minutes. Remove to wire racks; cool completely.

3. Beat butter and shortening in large bowl with electric mixer at medium speed until well blended. Add powdered sugar, ⅓ cup cream and salt; beat on low speed 1 minute. Beat on medium-high speed 2 minutes or until fluffy. Place filling in pastry bag fitted with large round tip. Stick tip into top of each cupcake and squeeze in a small amount of filling. Set remaining filling aside.

4. Place chocolate chips in medium heatproof bowl. Bring remaining 1 cup cream to a simmer in small saucepan over medium heat. Pour cream over chocolate chips; let stand 1 minute. Whisk until chocolate is melted and mixture is smooth.

5. Place wire rack over waxed paper. Dip tops of each cupcake into chocolate mixture; place on wire rack. Dip a second time, if desired. Let stand until set. Pipe swirl design on top of chocolate using remaining filling.

Makes 24 cupcakes

Fishy Friends

1 package (about 18 ounces) cake mix, any flavor, plus ingredients to prepare mix
1 container (16 ounces) white frosting
Orange, purple and blue food coloring
Assorted colored jelly candy fruit slices
Colored round gummy candies
White round candies
Black decorating gel

1. Preheat oven to 350°F. Line 22 standard (2½-inch) muffin cups with paper baking cups. Prepare cake mix according to package directions. Spoon batter into prepared muffin cups, filling two-thirds full.

2. Bake 20 minutes or until toothpick inserted into centers comes out clean. Cool in pans 10 minutes. Remove to wire racks; cool completely.

3. Divide frosting between three small bowls. Add food coloring, a few drops at a time, until desired shades are reached. Frost cupcakes.

4. Cut jelly candies into triangles for fins and tails. Arrange white candies and gummy candies at one end of each cupcake to create faces; add dot of decorating gel to each eye. Arrange jelly candy triangles on top and side of each cupcake.

Makes 22 cupcakes

Cubcakes

1 package (about 18 ounces) chocolate cake mix, plus ingredients to prepare mix
1 container (16 ounces) chocolate frosting
1 package (5 ounces) chocolate nonpareil candies
72 red cinnamon candies
Chocolate sprinkles
Black decorating gel

1. Preheat oven to 350°F. Line 22 standard (2½-inch) muffin cups with paper baking cups or spray with nonstick cooking spray. Prepare cake mix according to package directions. Spoon batter into prepared muffin cups, filling two-thirds full.

2. Bake 20 minutes or until toothpick inserted into centers comes out clean. Cool in pans 10 minutes. Remove to wire racks; cool completely.

3. Frost cupcakes with chocolate frosting. Use nonpareils to create ears and muzzle. Add cinnamon candies for eyes and noses. Decorate with chocolate sprinkles for fur. Use decorating gel to place dots on eyes and create mouth. *Makes 22 cupcakes*

Fishy Friends

Ooze Cupcakes

- 1 package (8 ounces) cream cheese, softened
- ½ cup powdered sugar
- ⅓ cup frozen limeade concentrate
- 1 teaspoon vanilla
- Yellow and blue food coloring
- 1 package (about 18 ounces) chocolate cake mix, plus ingredients to prepare mix
- 1 container (16 ounces) vanilla frosting
- Orange sugar

1. Preheat oven to 350°F. Line 24 standard (2½-inch) muffin cups with paper baking cups or spray with nonstick cooking spray.

2. Beat cream cheese, powdered sugar, limeade concentrate and vanilla in large bowl with electric mixer at medium speed 2 to 3 minutes or until well blended. Add yellow food coloring, a few drops at a time, until desired shade is reached. Set aside.

3. Prepare cake mix according to package directions, using only 1 egg. Spoon batter into prepared muffin cups, filling half full. Spoon 1 rounded teaspoon cream cheese mixture into center of each cup.

4. Bake 20 minutes or until toothpick inserted into centers comes out clean. Cool in pans 10 minutes. Remove to wire racks; cool completely.

5. Add 4 drops yellow food coloring and 2 drops blue food coloring to frosting in small bowl. Stir until well blended. Adjust color as needed by adding additional food coloring, 1 drop at a time, until desired shade is reached. Frost cupcakes; sprinkle with sugar.

Makes 24 cupcakes

Fortune Teller Cupcakes

- 1 package (about 18 ounces) dark chocolate cake mix, plus ingredients to prepare mix
- 1½ cups whipping cream
- 1 package (12 ounces) semisweet chocolate chips
- Black gel food coloring
- Prepared white frosting
- Black decorating gel

1. Preheat oven to 350°F. Line 24 standard (2½-inch) muffin cups with paper baking cups. Prepare cake mix according to package directions. Spoon batter into prepared muffin cups, filling two-thirds full.

2. Bake 20 minutes or until toothpick inserted into centers comes out clean. Cool in pans 10 minutes. Remove to wire racks; cool completely.

3. Bring cream to a simmer in small saucepan over medium heat. Place chocolate chips in medium bowl. Pour hot cream over chocolate chips; let stand 2 minutes. Whisk mixture until smooth. Add food coloring, a few drops at a time, to reach desired shade of black.

4. Place wire rack over waxed paper. Dip tops of cupcakes into chocolate mixture; place on wire rack. Allow to set; dip again, if desired. Pipe circles or triangle in center of each cupcake using frosting; smooth gently.

5. For numbered balls, pipe "8" in center of each white circle using decorating gel. For fortunes, pipe short messages like "yes" or "no" in center of each white triangle using decorating gel.

Makes 24 cupcakes

Yes
8

Sunny Side Upcakes

- 1 package (about 18 ounces) vanilla cake mix, plus ingredients to prepare mix
- 22 yellow chewy fruit candy squares
- 2 containers (16 ounces each) white frosting

1. Preheat oven to 350°F. Line 22 standard (2½-inch) muffin cups with paper baking cups. Prepare cake mix according to package directions. Spoon batter into prepared muffin cups, filling two-thirds full. Bake 20 minutes or until toothpick inserted into centers comes out clean. Cool in pans 10 minutes. Remove to wire racks; cool completely.

2. For each egg yolk, unwrap 1 candy square and microwave on LOW (30%) 5 seconds or just until softened. Shape into ball; flatten slightly.

3. Place 1 cup frosting in small microwavable bowl; microwave on LOW (30%) 10 seconds or until softened. Working with one cupcake at a time, spoon about 2 tablespoons frosting in center of cupcake. Spread frosting toward edges of cupcake in uneven petal shapes to resemble egg white. Press candy into frosting in center of cupcake. Microwave additional frosting as needed.

Makes 22 cupcakes

No-Bake Mini Cheesecakes

- 1 package (8 ounces) PHILADELPHIA® Cream Cheese, softened
- ½ cup sugar
- 1 tub (8 ounces) COOL WHIP® Whipped Topping, thawed
- 12 OREO® Chocolate Sandwich Cookies
- Multi-colored sprinkles (optional)

BEAT cream cheese and sugar until well blended. Gently stir in whipped topping.

PLACE cookies on bottom of 12 paper-lined muffin cups.

SPOON cream cheese mixture into muffin cups. Top with multi-colored sprinkles. Refrigerate until ready to serve.

Makes 12 servings

Prep Time: 10 minutes

Sunny Side Upcakes

Dinocakes

1 package (about 18 ounces) chocolate fudge or devil's food cake mix, plus ingredients to prepare mix

44 long chewy chocolate candies (3×¼ inch), divided

10 to 15 small chewy chocolate candies

1 container (16 ounces) chocolate frosting

Candy sprinkles and decorating decors

1. Preheat oven to 350°F. Line 22 standard (2½-inch) muffin cups with paper baking cups. Prepare cake mix according to package directions. Spoon batter into prepared muffin cups, filling two-thirds full.

2. Bake 20 minutes or until toothpick inserted into centers comes out clean. Cool in pans 10 minutes. Remove to wire racks; cool completely.

3. Shape 22 long candies into dinosaur heads. (If candies are too stiff to bend, microwave on LOW (30%) 6 to 8 seconds to soften.)

4. Cut about 1 inch from remaining 22 long candies with scissors; shape each into pointed tail. Make 4 to 5 small cuts along length of candies, being careful not to cut all the way through. Curve candies into tail shape. Press and flatten small candies into rectangles; cut rectangles into small triangles for dinosaur spikes.

5. Frost cupcakes. Press candy head and tail into opposite sides of each cupcake; arrange candy triangles in between. Decorate with sprinkles; press decors into dinosaur heads for eyes.

Makes 22 cupcakes

Blue Suede Cupcakes

- 2¼ cups all-purpose flour
- 1 teaspoon salt
- 2 bottles (1 ounce each) blue food coloring
- 3 tablespoons unsweetened cocoa powder
- 1 cup buttermilk
- 1 teaspoon vanilla
- 1½ cups granulated sugar
- 1 cup (2 sticks) unsalted butter, softened, divided
- 2 eggs
- 1 teaspoon white vinegar
- 1 teaspoon baking soda
- 1 package (8 ounces) cream cheese
- 3 cups powdered sugar
- 2 tablespoons milk
- Additional blue food coloring
- Blue decorating sugar (optional)

1. Preheat oven to 350°F. Line 20 standard (2½-inch) muffin cups with paper baking cups.

2. Whisk flour and salt in medium bowl. Gradually stir food coloring into cocoa in small bowl until blended and smooth. Combine buttermilk and vanilla in another small bowl.

3. Beat granulated sugar and ½ cup butter in large bowl with electric mixer at medium speed 4 minutes or until light and fluffy. Add eggs, one at a time, beating well after each addition. Add cocoa mixture; beat until well blended and uniform in color. Add flour mixture alternately with buttermilk mixture, beating just until blended. Stir vinegar into baking soda in small bowl; gently fold into batter (do not use mixer). Spoon batter evenly into prepared muffin cups, filling half full.

4. Bake 20 minutes or until toothpick inserted into centers comes out clean. Cool in pans 10 minutes. Remove to wire racks; cool completely.

5. Beat remaining ½ cup butter and cream cheese in large bowl with electric mixer at medium-high speed until smooth. Gradually beat in powdered sugar at low speed. Beat in milk until blended. Tint with additional food coloring, if desired. Pipe or spread frosting over cupcakes. Sprinkle with decorating sugar, if desired.

Makes 20 cupcakes

Zebra Stripes

1 package (about 18 ounces) dark chocolate cake mix, plus ingredients to prepare mix
24 ounces white chocolate, chopped
8 ounces whipping cream
Black decorating icing

1. Preheat oven to 350°F. Line 24 standard (2½-inch) muffin cups with paper baking cups. Prepare cake mix according to package directions. Spoon batter evenly into prepared muffin cups. Bake 20 minutes or until toothpick inserted into centers comes out clean. Cool in pans 10 minutes. Remove to rack; cool completely.

2. Place white chocolate in medium bowl. Bring cream to a simmer in small saucepan over medium heat; pour over white chocolate. Let stand 5 minutes. Stir until smooth.

3. Place wire racks over waxed paper. Dip tops of cupcakes in white chocolate mixture. Transfer to wire racks; let stand 10 minutes or until set. Pipe stripes on tops of cupcakes using black decorating icing. *Makes 24 cupcakes*

Meteorite Mini Cakes

1 package (about 18 ounces) chocolate cake mix, plus ingredients to prepare mix
2 containers (16 ounces each) vanilla frosting
Red, green, blue and yellow food coloring
1 bag (11 ounces) chocolate chunks

1. Preheat oven to 350°F. Spray 12 standard (2½-inch) muffin cups with nonstick cooking spray. Prepare cake mix according to package directions. Spoon batter evenly into prepared muffin cups. Bake 20 minutes or until toothpick inserted into centers comes out clean. Cool in pan on wire rack placed over sheet of waxed paper 10 minutes. Remove to rack; cool completely.

2. Trim cupcakes to form irregular shapes. Microwave frosting in medium microwavable bowl on LOW (30%) about 30 seconds or until melted. Divide frosting between small bowls and tint with food coloring. Pour half of frosting from each bowl over cupcakes, coating completely.

3. Refrigerate cakes 20 minutes. Press chocolate chunks into frosting to create bumpy surface. Melt remaining frosting; coat cupcakes again. Chill until ready to serve. *Makes 12 cakes*

Zebra Stripes

Billiard Ball Cupcakes

- 1 package (about 18 ounces) cake mix, any flavor, plus ingredients to prepare mix
- 6 cups powdered sugar, divided
- 1 cup (2 sticks) unsalted butter, softened
- 6 to 8 tablespoons milk, divided
- 1 teaspoon vanilla
- Assorted gel food coloring
- White wafer candy discs
- Black decorating gel

1. Preheat oven to 350°F. Line 24 standard (2½-inch) muffin cups with paper baking cups. Prepare cake mix according to package directions. Spoon batter evenly into prepared muffin cups.

2. Bake 20 minutes or until toothpick inserted into centers comes out clean. Cool in pans 10 minutes. Remove to rack; cool completely.

3. Combine 3 cups powdered sugar, butter, 4 tablespoons milk and vanilla in large bowl. Beat with electric mixer at low speed until smooth. Add remaining 3 cups powdered sugar; beat until light and fluffy, adding remaining milk, 1 tablespoon at a time, as needed for spreadable consistency.

4. Reserve one fourth of frosting. Divide remaining frosting evenly among small bowls and tint with food coloring to make desired colors. For "solids," frost cupcakes with colored frosting. Place one candy disc in center of each cupcake.

5. For "stripes," frost cupcakes with reserved white frosting. Spread center two thirds of each cupcake with tinted frosting. Place one candy disc in center of each cupcake.

6. Pipe number in center of each candy disc using decorating gel.

Makes 24 cupcakes

Pink Piglets

- 1 package (about 18 ounces) yellow cake mix, plus ingredients to prepare mix
- 1 container (16 ounces) white frosting
- Pink or red food coloring
- Mini semisweet chocolate chips
- Small fruit-flavored pastel candy wafers
- Red or pink chewy fruit candy squares

1. Preheat oven to 350°F. Line 60 mini (1¾-inch) muffin cups with paper baking cups. Prepare cake mix according to package directions. Spoon batter evenly into prepared muffin cups, filling almost full.

2. Bake 10 minutes or until toothpick inserted into centers comes out clean. Cool in pans 10 minutes. Remove to wire racks; cool completely.

3. Place frosting in medium bowl; add food coloring, a few drops at a time, until desired shade of pink is reached. Frost cupcakes. Create faces at one end of each cupcake using chocolate chips for eyes and candy wafers for noses.

4. Working with one at a time, unwrap candy squares and microwave on LOW (30%) 5 to 10 seconds or until softened. Press candies between hands or on waxed paper to flatten to ⅛-inch thickness. Use scissors or paring knife to cut out triangles for ears; fold over top corner of each triangle. Arrange ears on cupcakes.

5. Cut ⅛-inch strips, 1 to 2 inches long, from flattened candies. Shape candy strips into spirals for tails; place candies in freezer 10 minutes to set. Place tails on cupcakes. *Makes 60 piglets*

Whoopie Pie Cupcakes

- 1 package (about 18 ounces) dark chocolate cake mix, plus ingredients to prepare mix
- ½ cup (1 stick) unsalted butter, softened
- ¼ cup shortening
- 3 cups powdered sugar
- ⅓ cup whipping cream
- 1 teaspoon salt

1. Preheat oven to 350°F. Grease 24 standard (2½-inch) muffin cups. Prepare cake mix according to package directions. Spoon batter into prepared muffin cups, filling two-thirds full. Bake 20 minutes or until toothpick inserted into centers comes out clean. Cool in pans 10 minutes. Remove to wire racks; cool completely.
2. Beat butter and shortening in large bowl with electric mixer at medium speed until well blended. Add powdered sugar, cream and salt; beat at low speed 1 minute. Beat at medium-high speed 2 minutes or until fluffy.
3. Slice tops off cupcakes. Spread filling over bottoms of cupcakes; replace tops.

Makes 24 cupcakes

Colossal Birthday Cupcake

- 1 package (about 18 ounces) devil's food cake mix, plus ingredients to prepare mix
- 1 container (16 ounces) vanilla or chocolate frosting, divided
- ¼ cup peanut butter
- Construction paper or aluminum foil
- Fruit-flavored candy wafers or chocolate shavings

1. Preheat oven to 350°F. Grease and flour two 8-inch round cake pans.
2. Prepare cake mix according to package directions; spread batter into prepared pans. Bake 30 minutes or until toothpick inserted into centers comes out clean. Cool completely in pans.
3. Beat ¾ cup frosting and peanut butter in medium bowl. Place one cake layer on serving plate; spread evenly with peanut butter frosting. Top with second cake layer; spread top with remaining vanilla frosting, mounding frosting slightly higher in center.
4. Cut 36×3½-inch piece of construction paper; pleat paper every ½ inch. Wrap around side of cake to resemble baking cup. Decorate with candy wafers.

Makes 12 servings

Whoopie Pie Cupcakes

Sweet Little Sheep

- 1 package (about 18 ounces) cake mix, any flavor, plus ingredients to prepare mix
- 1 container (16 ounces) white frosting
- 2 packages (10½ ounces each) mini marshmallows
- Chewy chocolate candies
- Small white and pink round decors
- Black decorating gel

1. Preheat oven to 350°F. Line 60 mini (1¾-inch) muffin cups with paper baking cups. Prepare cake mix according to package directions. Spoon batter into prepared muffin cups, filling almost full.

2. Bake 10 minutes or until toothpick inserted into centers comes out clean. Cool in pans 10 minutes. Remove to wire racks; cool completely.

3. Frost cupcakes. Press marshmallows into frosting, completely covering cupcakes.

4. Unwrap chewy chocolate candies; cut off small piece of each candy and reserve. Working with one large piece at a time, microwave on LOW (30%) 5 seconds or until slightly softened. For heads, press candy between hands or on waxed paper to flatten slightly; form into oblong shape. For ears, cut reserved small pieces of candy in half. Shape each half into triangle.

5. Place candy head on one side of each cupcake. Attach decors for eyes, noses and ears to head using small dabs of frosting. Add dot of gel to each eye.

Makes 60 sheep

Orange Dreamsicle Cupcakes

1½ cups all-purpose flour
1½ (0.15-ounce) envelopes orange unsweetened drink mix
2 teaspoons baking powder
⅛ teaspoon salt
1 cup granulated sugar
1 cup (2 sticks) unsalted butter, softened, divided
2 eggs
½ cup plus 3 tablespoons milk, divided
1½ teaspoons vanilla, divided
3 cups powdered sugar
Orange gel food coloring
White sprinkles (optional)

1. Preheat oven to 350°F. Line 12 standard (2½-inch) muffin cups with paper baking cups.

2. Whisk flour, drink mix, baking powder and salt in small bowl. Beat granulated sugar and ½ cup butter in medium bowl with electric mixer at medium speed until creamy. Add eggs, one at a time, beating well after each addition. Add flour mixture; beat until blended. Add ½ cup milk and 1 teaspoon vanilla; beat until smooth.

3. Divide batter evenly into prepared muffin cups. Bake 20 minutes or until toothpick inserted into centers comes out clean. Cool in pan 10 minutes. Remove to wire rack; cool completely.

4. Meanwhile, beat powdered sugar, remaining ½ cup butter, 3 tablespoons milk and ½ teaspoon vanilla in large bowl at medium speed until fluffy. Tint with food coloring. Pipe or spread onto cupcakes. Decorate with sprinkles, if desired.

Makes 12 cupcakes

All Dressed Up

Limoncello Cupcakes

Cupcakes

- 1 package (about 18 ounces) lemon cake mix
- 4 eggs
- 1 package (4-serving size) lemon instant pudding and pie filling mix
- ½ cup vegetable oil
- ½ cup vodka
- ½ cup water

Glaze

- 4 cups powdered sugar
- ⅓ cup lemon juice
- 3 to 4 tablespoons vodka
- Candied lemon peel
- Coarse sugar (optional)

1. Preheat oven to 350°F. Line 24 standard (2½-inch) muffin cups with paper baking cups.

2. Beat cake mix, eggs, pudding mix, oil, ½ cup vodka and water in large bowl with electric mixer at low speed until smooth. Spoon batter evenly into prepared muffin cups. Bake 15 minutes or until toothpick inserted into centers comes out clean. Cool completely in pans on wire racks.

3. For glaze, whisk powdered sugar, lemon juice and 3 tablespoons vodka in medium bowl until smooth. Add remaining 1 tablespoon vodka if icing is too stiff. Dip tops of cupcakes in glaze; garnish with candied lemon peel. Sprinkle with coarse sugar, if desired. Let stand until set.

Makes 24 cupcakes

Mini Praline Cakes

- 1½ cups PLANTERS® Chopped Pecans
- ½ cup (1 stick) butter or margarine, melted
- ½ cup firmly packed brown sugar
- 1 package (16 ounces) pound cake mix
- ½ cup water
- ½ cup BREAKSTONE'S® or KNUDSEN® Sour Cream
- 2 eggs
- 1½ cups caramel ice cream topping
- 1½ cups thawed COOL WHIP® Whipped Topping

HEAT oven to 350°F. Combine pecans, butter and sugar; spoon into 24 well-greased and floured 2½-inch muffin cups. Beat cake mix, water, sour cream and eggs with mixer 3 minutes. Spoon into cups.

BAKE 15 to 18 minutes or until toothpick inserted in centers comes out clean. Cool in pans on wire racks 15 minutes. Carefully loosen cakes and invert to remove from pans; cool completely.

DRIZZLE with caramel topping just before serving. Top with whipped topping. *Makes 24 cakes*

Make Ahead: Cakes can be stored in refrigerator up to 3 days before topping as directed and serving.

Prep Time: 20 minutes
Total Time: 1 hour 8 minutes (including cooling)

Blueberry Cupcakes with Goat Cheese Frosting

Cupcakes

- 1½ cups all-purpose flour
- 1¾ teaspoons baking powder
- ½ teaspoon salt
- ¾ cup granulated sugar
- ½ cup (1 stick) unsalted butter, softened
- 2 eggs
- 2 teaspoons vanilla
- ½ cup milk
- 1 cup blueberries, plus additional for garnish

Goat Cheese Frosting

- 4 ounces goat cheese
- ¼ cup (½ stick) unsalted butter, softened
- 2 cups powdered sugar
- 2 tablespoons milk

1. Preheat oven to 350°F. Line 12 standard (2½-inch) muffin cups with paper baking cups. Whisk flour, baking powder and salt in small bowl.

2. Beat ½ cup butter and granulated sugar in large bowl with electric mixer at medium speed until light and fluffy. Add eggs and vanilla; beat well. Add flour mixture and ½ cup milk; beat at low speed just until combined. Stir in blueberries. Spoon batter evenly into prepared muffin cups.

3. Bake 20 minutes or until toothpick inserted into centers comes out clean. Cool in pans 10 minutes. Remove to wire rack; cool completely.

4. For frosting, beat goat cheese and ¼ cup butter in large bowl with electric mixer at medium speed until well blended. Add powdered sugar and 2 tablespoons milk; beat until smooth. Frost cupcakes; garnish with fresh blueberries. *Makes 12 cupcakes*

Boston Cream Pie Minis

- 1 package (2-layer size) yellow cake mix
- 1 cup cold milk
- 1 package (4-serving size) JELL-O® Vanilla Flavor Instant Pudding & Pie Filling
- 1½ cups thawed COOL WHIP® Whipped Topping, divided
- 4 squares BAKER'S® Semi-Sweet Baking Chocolate

PREHEAT oven to 350°F. Prepare cake batter and bake in 24 greased medium muffin pan cups as directed on package. Cool 10 minutes in pans. Remove to wire racks; cool completely.

BEAT milk and dry pudding mix with wire whisk 2 minutes or until well blended. Let stand 5 minutes. Meanwhile, use serrated knife to cut cupcakes horizontally in half. Gently stir ½ cup of the whipped topping into pudding. Spoon about 1 tablespoon of the pudding mixture onto bottom half of each cupcake; cover with top of cupcake.

MICROWAVE remaining 1 cup whipped topping and the chocolate in small microwaveable bowl on high 1½ minutes or until chocolate is almost melted, stirring after 1 minute. Stir until chocolate is completely melted and mixture is well blended; spread onto cupcakes. Refrigerate at least 15 minutes before serving. Store leftovers in refrigerator. *Makes 24 cupcakes*

Prep Time: 15 minutes

Tip

The classic flavors of Boston Cream Pie, with its custardy filling and rich chocolate glaze, have been scaled down to create the perfect dinner party dessert. You can forget about messy slicing and plating when you serve these adorable single-serving minis to your guests.

Spicy Chocolate Cupcakes

- 2½ cups all-purpose flour
- 1 teaspoon baking soda
- 1 teaspoon baking powder
- 1 teaspoon ground cinnamon
- ½ teaspoon salt
- ⅛ teaspoon ground nutmeg
- 1½ cups sugar
- ¾ cup (1½ sticks) unsalted butter, softened
- 3 eggs
- 1½ teaspoons vanilla
- 1 container (7 ounces) plain Greek yogurt
- 2 tablespoons canola or vegetable oil
- Spicy Chocolate Frosting (recipe follows)
- Chocolate curls (optional)

1. Preheat oven to 350°F. Line 24 standard (2½-inch) muffin cups with paper baking cups.

2. Whisk flour, baking soda, baking powder, cinnamon, salt and nutmeg in medium bowl. Beat sugar and butter in large bowl with electric mixer at medium speed until creamy. Add eggs and vanilla, beating until well blended. Alternately add flour mixture, yogurt and oil to butter mixture, beating well after each addition. Pour batter evenly into prepared muffin cups.

3. Bake 18 minutes or until toothpick inserted into centers comes out clean. Cool in pans 10 minutes. Remove to wire racks; cool completely.

4. Meanwhile, prepare Spicy Chocolate Frosting. Pipe or spread onto cupcakes. Garnish with chocolate curls, if desired.

Makes 24 cupcakes

Spicy Chocolate Frosting: Beat 2 cups (4 sticks) softened unsalted butter in large bowl with electric mixer at medium speed until creamy. Add 4 cups powdered sugar, ¼ cup milk, 1 teaspoon cinnamon, 1 teaspoon ancho chile powder, 1 teaspoon vanilla and ½ teaspoon ground red pepper; beat until fluffy. Beat in 10 ounces cooled melted bittersweet (70%) chocolate until blended. Makes about 4 cups.

Mini Lemon Cheesecakes

- 40 NILLA® Wafers, finely crushed (about 1⅔ cups crumbs)
- ¼ cup (½ stick) butter or margarine, softened
- 3 teaspoon grated lemon peel, divided
- 1 package (8 ounces) PHILADELPHIA® Cream Cheese, softened
- ½ cup sugar
- 1 egg
- 1 tablespoon lemon juice

PREHEAT oven to 350°F. Mix wafer crumbs, butter and 2 teaspoons of the lemon peel until well blended. Spoon about 2 tablespoons of the crumb mixture into each of 12 greased or paper-lined medium muffin cups. Press crumb mixture firmly onto bottom and up side of each cup to form crust.

BEAT cream cheese with electric mixer on medium speed until creamy. Gradually add sugar and remaining 1 teaspoon lemon peel, beating after each addition until well blended. Add egg and lemon juice; beat just until blended. Spoon batter evenly into crusts.

BAKE 40 minutes or until lightly browned. Turn oven off. Let cheesecakes stand in oven for 20 minutes, leaving door slightly ajar. Remove to wire rack to cool. Refrigerate at least 1 hour before serving.

REMOVE from paper liners before serving. Store leftover cheesecakes in refrigerator. *Makes 12 servings*

Prep Time: 30 minutes plus refrigerating
Bake Time: 40 minutes

Maple Bacon Cupcakes

Cupcakes

- 1½ cups all-purpose flour
- 1¾ teaspoons baking powder
- ½ cup (1 stick) unsalted butter, softened
- ¾ cup granulated sugar
- 2 eggs
- 2 tablespoons maple syrup
- ½ cup milk
- 8 slices bacon, crisp-cooked and finely chopped, divided

Maple Frosting

- ½ cup (1 stick) unsalted butter, softened
- 3 tablespoons maple syrup
- 2 tablespoons milk
- 3 cups powdered sugar

1. Preheat oven to 350°F. Line 12 standard (2½-inch) muffin cups with paper baking cups. Whisk flour and baking powder in small bowl.

2. Beat ½ cup butter and granulated sugar in large bowl with electric mixer at medium speed until light and fluffy. Add eggs and 2 tablespoons maple syrup; beat well. Add flour mixture and ½ cup milk; beat at low speed just until combined. Stir in all but 2 tablespoons chopped bacon.

3. Spoon batter evenly into prepared muffin cups. Bake 20 minutes or until toothpick inserted into centers comes out clean. Cool in pan 10 minutes. Remove to wire rack; cool completely.

4. For frosting, beat ½ cup butter, 3 tablespoons maple syrup and 2 tablespoons milk in large bowl with electric mixer at low speed 1 minute. Add powdered sugar; beat at medium speed until fluffy. Frost cupcakes; top with reserved chopped bacon.

Makes 12 cupcakes

Brownie Bon Bons

- 2 jars (10 ounces each) maraschino cherries with stems
- Cherry liqueur (optional)*
- 4 squares BAKER'S® Unsweetened Baking Chocolate
- ¾ cup (1½ sticks) butter *or* margarine
- 2 cups granulated sugar
- 4 eggs
- 1 teaspoon vanilla
- 1 cup flour
- Chocolate Fudge Filling (recipe follows)
- ½ cup powdered sugar

**For liqueur-flavored cherries, drain liquid from cherries. Do not remove cherries from jars. Refill jars with liqueur to completely cover cherries; cover tightly. Let stand at least 24 hours for best flavor.*

HEAT oven to 350°F.

MICROWAVE chocolate and butter in large microwavable bowl on HIGH 2 minutes or until butter is melted. Stir until chocolate is completely melted.

STIR granulated sugar into chocolate mixture until well blended. Mix in eggs and vanilla. Stir in flour until well blended. Spoon into greased 1¾×1-inch muffin cups filling each cup ⅔ full.

BAKE for 20 minutes or until toothpick inserted into center comes out with fudgy crumbs. DO NOT OVERBAKE. Cool slightly in muffin pans; loosen edges with tip of knife. Remove from pans. Turn each brownie onto wax paper-lined tray while warm. Make ½-inch indentation into top of each brownie "bon bon" with end of wooden spoon. Cool completely.

MEANWHILE prepare Chocolate Fudge Filling. Drain cherries, reserving liqueur. Let cherries stand on paper towels to allow surfaces to dry. Mix powdered sugar with enough reserved liqueur to form a thin glaze.

PIPE or spoon about 1 teaspoon Chocolate Fudge Filling into indentation of each brownie to assemble bon bons. Gently press cherry into filling. Drizzle with powdered sugar glaze.

Makes about 48 bon bons

Chocolate Fudge Filling

- 3 squares BAKER'S® Unsweetened Baking Chocolate
- 4 ounces (½ of 8-ounce package) PHILADELPHIA® Cream Cheese, softened
- 1 teaspoon vanilla
- ¼ cup light corn syrup
- 1 cup powdered sugar

MICROWAVE chocolate in small microwavable bowl on HIGH 1 to 2 minutes or until chocolate is almost melted. Stir until chocolate is completely melted. Cool.

BEAT cream cheese and vanilla in small bowl with electric mixer on medium speed until smooth. Gradually add corn syrup, beating until well blended.

BEAT in chocolate until smooth. Gradually add powdered sugar, beating until well blended and smooth. *Makes about 1 cup*

Banana Cream Pie Cupcakes

- 1 package (about 18 ounces) yellow cake mix, plus ingredients to prepare mix
- 1 package (4-serving size) banana instant pudding and pie filling mix
- 2 cups cold milk
- 2 bananas
- 2 tablespoons sugar, divided
- 2 cups cold whipping cream

1. Preheat oven to 350°F. Line 24 standard (2½-inch) muffin cups with paper baking cups. Prepare cake mix according to package directions. Spoon batter into prepared muffin cups, filling two-thirds full.

2. Bake 20 minutes or until toothpick inserted into centers comes out clean. Cool in pans 10 minutes. Remove to wire racks; cool completely.

3. Prepare pudding using milk according to package directions. Refrigerate until set.

4. Preheat broiler. Line baking sheet with parchment paper. Slice each banana into 12 slices. Place 1 tablespoon sugar onto plate. Dip one side of banana slice into sugar; place sugar side up onto prepared baking sheet. Broil 2 minutes or just until bananas start to turn light golden brown; remove from broiler immediately. Cool completely.

5. Beat whipping cream and remaining 1 tablespoon sugar in large bowl with electric mixer at medium-high speed until stiff peaks form.

6. Using a sharp knife, cut out 1-inch hole in top of each cupcake. Fill with pudding; save remaining pudding for another use. Using piping bag fitted with large star tip, pipe whipped cream onto cupcakes. Top each with banana slice. *Makes 24 cupcakes*

Caramel-Topped Cheesecakes with Oat-Pecan Crust

- 1½ cups QUAKER® Oats (quick or old fashioned), uncooked
- ½ cup finely chopped pecans
- 1¼ cups packed light brown sugar, divided
- ¼ cup butter or margarine, melted
- 2 packages (8 ounces each) cream cheese, softened
- 1 teaspoon vanilla
- 3 large eggs, at room temperature
- ½ cup sour cream
- ¾ cup butterscotch caramel topping
- Sea salt

1. Heat oven to 375°F. Line 18 medium muffin cups with foil liners.

2. Combine oats, pecans, ½ cup brown sugar and butter in large bowl, blending well. Spoon about 2 tablespoons of mixture into bottom of each foil-lined muffin cup, then press evenly and firmly to form crust. Bake 8 to 10 minutes, or until golden brown. Remove from oven and cool.

3. Reduce oven temperature to 325°F. Beat cream cheese in large bowl with electric mixer at medium-high speed until light and fluffy, scraping bowl occasionally. Add remaining ¾ cup brown sugar and vanilla; blend well. Add eggs, one at a time, beating just until blended. Add sour cream; mix well. Divide batter evenly among prepared muffin cups. Bake about 20 to 22 minutes, or just until set. Cool in pans on wire rack. Chill at least 2 hours.

4. Just before serving, top each individual cheesecake with scant tablespoon of butterscotch caramel topping (if too thick to spread, place in microwave for a few seconds to soften). Sprinkle on a few grains of sea salt and serve. *Makes 18 cheesecakes*

Jelly Doughnut Bites

- ½ cup plus 3 tablespoons warm (95 to 105°F) milk, divided
- 1¼ teaspoons active dry yeast
- ⅓ cup granulated sugar
- 1 tablespoon butter, softened
- 2½ cups all purpose flour
- 1 egg
- ½ teaspoon salt
- ½ cup raspberry jam
- Powdered sugar

1. Combine 3 tablespoons warm milk and yeast in large bowl of electric mixer. Stir; let stand 5 minutes. Add granulated sugar, butter and remaining ½ cup milk; mix well. Add flour, egg and salt; beat with dough hook at medium speed until dough starts to climb up dough hook. If dough is too sticky, add additional flour 1 tablespoon at a time.
2. Transfer dough to greased medium bowl; turn dough over to grease top. Cover bowl; let stand in warm place 1 hour.
3. Grease 48 mini (1¾-inch) muffin cups. Punch down dough. Pull off pieces of dough. Shape into 1-inch balls; place in prepared muffin cups. Cover; let stand 1 hour.
4. Preheat oven to 375°F. Uncover; bake 10 to 12 minutes or until light golden brown. Remove to wire rack; cool completely.
5. Place jam in piping bag fitted with round tip. Insert tip into side of doughnut; squeeze about 1 teaspoon jam into center. Dust filled doughnuts with powdered sugar.

Makes 48 doughnut bites

Tip: These doughnuts are best eaten the same day they are made. They can be served warm or at room temperature. If desired, heat 10 seconds in microwave right before serving.

Cannoli Cupcakes

- 2 cups all-purpose flour
- ½ teaspoon baking soda
- ½ teaspoon baking powder
- ½ teaspoon salt
- 1 cup granulated sugar
- ½ cup (1 stick) unsalted butter, softened
- 1 cup whole-milk ricotta cheese
- 1 teaspoon grated orange peel
- 1 egg
- 2 teaspoons vanilla, divided
- 1 cup whipping cream
- 8 ounces mascarpone cheese, softened
- ½ cup powdered sugar
- Mini semisweet chocolate chips and chopped unsalted pistachios (optional)

1. Preheat oven to 350°F. Line 15 standard (2½-inch) muffin cups with paper baking cups.

2. Whisk flour, baking soda, baking powder and salt in small bowl. Beat granulated sugar and butter in large bowl with electric mixer at medium speed until creamy. Add ricotta cheese and orange peel; beat until blended. Add egg and 1 teaspoon vanilla; beat until blended. Add flour mixture; beat until blended. Scoop batter evenly into prepared muffin cups.

3. Bake 20 minutes or until toothpick inserted into centers comes out clean. Cool in pans 10 minutes. Remove to wire racks; cool completely.

4. Meanwhile, beat cream in medium bowl at high speed until stiff peaks form. Stir together mascarpone cheese, powdered sugar and remaining 1 teaspoon vanilla in another medium bowl. Fold whipped cream into mascarpone mixture until blended. Pipe or spread onto cupcakes. Garnish with chocolate chips and pistachios.

Makes 15 cupcakes

Lemon Poppy Seed Cupcakes

1½ packages (12 ounces) cream cheese, softened
1½ cups plus ⅓ cup powdered sugar, divided
1 package (about 18 ounces) lemon cake mix, plus ingredients to prepare mix
1 tablespoon poppy seeds
Grated peel and juice of 1 lemon
Candied violets (optional)

1. Preheat oven to 350°F. Line 18 standard (2½-inch) muffin cups with paper baking cups.

2. Beat cream cheese and ⅓ cup powdered sugar in medium bowl with electric mixer at medium speed 1 minute or until light and fluffy.

3. Prepare cake mix according to package directions; stir in poppy seeds. Spoon 2 tablespoons batter into each prepared muffin cup. Place 2 teaspoons cream cheese mixture in center of each cup; cover with another 2 tablespoons batter.

4. Bake 22 to 24 minutes. Cool in pans 10 minutes. Remove to wire racks; cool completely.

5. Combine remaining 1½ cups powdered sugar, lemon peel and lemon juice in small bowl. Dip tops of cupcakes into glaze. Top with candied violet, if desired. *Makes 18 cupcakes*

Lemon Blueberry Shortcakes

24 REYNOLDS® Foil Baking Cups
1 package (18.25 ounces) vanilla or yellow cake mix
1 jar (10 ounces) lemon curd
1 container (8 ounces) frozen whipped topping, thawed, divided
Fresh blueberries or raspberries

Preheat oven to 350°F. Place REYNOLDS® Foil Baking Cups on cookie sheet with sides; set aside. Prepare cake mix following package directions for 24 cupcakes. Spoon cake batter into baking cups.

Bake 17 to 22 minutes. Cool. Mix lemon curd and 1 cup whipped topping in a medium bowl until well blended; set aside.

Cut the top off of each shortcake; set aside. Spoon about 1 tablespoon lemon mixture onto each shortcake; top with blueberries. Place top of shortcake over blueberries. Serve with remaining whipped topping. *Makes 24 servings*

Lemon Poppy Seed Cupcakes

Acknowledgments

The publisher would like to thank the companies and organizations listed below for the use of their recipes and photographs in this publication.

Campbell Soup Company

Cherry Marketing Institute

The Hershey Company

Kraft Foods Global, Inc.

© Mars, Incorporated 2011

Nestlé USA

Polaner®, A Division of B&G Foods, Inc.

The Quaker® Oatmeal Kitchens

Recipes courtesy of the Reynolds Kitchens

Index

A

All-American Cupcakes, 66

Almond Bark
- Dragonflies, 46
- Mini Fireworks, 48
- Sweet Snowflakes, 132

Animals
- Black Cat Cupcakes, 86
- Colorful Caterpillar Cupcakes, 52
- Cubcakes, 196
- Dinocakes, 204
- Dragonflies, 46
- Easter Chicks, 16
- Fishy Friends, 196
- Friendly Frogs, 30
- Funny Bunnies, 34
- Leopard Spots, 192
- Little Lamb Cakes, 40
- Mini Bees, 42
- Monkey A-Rounds, 174
- Panda Cupcakes, 190
- Pink Piglets, 212
- Pupcakes, 192
- Snowy Owl Cupcakes, 118
- Sweet Little Sheep, 216
- Under the Sea, 68
- Zebra Stripes, 208

Apple
- Apple Cider Cupcakes, 76
- Apple Cider Frosting, 76
- Apple Glaze, 84
- Caramel Apple Cupcakes, 102

Apple *(continued)*
- Glazed Applesauce Spice Cakes, 84
- Taffy Apple Cupcakes, 90

Apple Cider Cupcakes, 76

Apple Cider Frosting, 76

Apple Glaze, 84

B

Bacon: Maple Bacon Cupcakes, 232

Banana
- Banana Cream Pie Cupcakes, 236
- Dark Chocolate Banana Cupcakes, 150
- Tropical Luau Cupcakes, 64

Banana Cream Pie Cupcakes, 236

Billiard Ball Cupcakes, 210

Black Cat Cupcakes, 86

Blue Suede Cupcakes, 206

Blueberries
- Blueberry Cupcakes with Goat Cheese Frosting, 224
- Lemon Blueberry Shortcakes, 244

Blueberry Cupcakes with Goat Cheese Frosting, 224

Boston Cream Pie Minis, 226

Browned Butter Frosting, 134

Brownie Bon Bons, 234

Brownies
- Brownie Bon Bons, 234
- Coffee Brownie Bites, 164
- Feathered Friends, 100
- Mini Brownie Cups, 178
- Touchdown Brownie Cups, 92
- Truffle Brownie Bites, 154

Butter Pecan Cupcakes, 134

Buttercream Frosting, 146

Butterscotch Chips: Glazed Applesauce Spice Cakes, 84

C

Cake Mix, Any Flavor
- All-American Cupcakes, 66
- Billiard Ball Cupcakes, 210
- Black Cat Cupcakes, 86
- Dragonflies, 46
- Fishy Friends, 196
- Friendly Frogs, 30
- I Think You're "Marbleous" Cupcakes, 124
- Sweet Little Sheep, 216
- Under the Sea, 68

Cake Mix, Chocolate
- Cherry Cupcakes, 48
- Chocolate Easter Baskets, 20
- Chocolate Moose, 160
- Chocolate Tiramisu Cupcakes, 184

Index

Cake Mix, Chocolate *(continued)*
- Cream Cheese Surprise Cupcakes, 168
- Cubcakes, 196
- Halloween Hedgehogs, 92
- Magically Minty Mini Cupcakes, 36
- Meteorite Mini Cakes, 208
- Mini Bees, 42
- Mini Fireworks, 48
- Mini Oreo® Surprise Cupcakes, 156
- Monkey A-Rounds, 174
- Mummy Cakes, 96
- Ooze Cupcakes, 198
- Pupcakes, 192
- Snowy Peaks, 114

Cake Mix, Chocolate Fudge
- Dinocakes, 204
- Iced Coffee Cupcakes, 152
- Rocky Road Cupcakes, 168
- Triple Chocolate PB Minis, 172

Cake Mix, Dark Chocolate
- Cappuccino Cupcakes, 88
- Chocolate Sweetheart Cupcakes, 118
- Cream-Filled Cupcakes, 194
- Fortune Teller Cupcakes, 200
- Individual Flower Pot Cakes, 32
- Leopard Spots, 192

Cake Mix, Dark Chocolate *(continued)*
- Peppermint Mocha Cupcakes, 142
- Whoopie Pie Cupcakes, 214
- Zebra Stripes, 208

Cake Mix, Devil's Food: Colossal Birthday Cupcake, 214

Cake Mix, German Chocolate: German Chocolate Cupcakes, 180

Cake Mix, Lemon
- Key Lime Pie Cupcakes, 18
- Lemon Meringue Cupcakes, 38
- Lemon Poppy Seed Cupcakes, 244
- Limoncello Cupcakes, 220

Cake Mix, Pound
- Hot Chocolate Cupcakes, 28
- Mini Praline Cakes, 222
- Polka Dot Pumpkin Cupcakes, 86

Cake Mix, Spice: Apple Cider Cupcakes, 76

Cake Mix, Strawberry: Strawberry Preserve Cupcakes, 70

Cake Mix, Vanilla
- Colorful Caterpillar Cupcakes, 52
- Lemon Blueberry Shortcakes, 244

Cake Mix, Vanilla *(continued)*
- Sunny Side Upcakes, 202
- Sweet Snowmen, 122

Cake Mix, White
- Chai Latte Cupcakes, 144
- Christmas Tree Cupcakes, 146
- Graduation Party Cupcakes, 58
- Holiday Poke Cupcakes, 132
- Ice Cream Cone Cupcakes, 58
- Lemon-Cream Cheese Cupcakes, 28
- Lovin' Sweetcakes, 142
- Margarita Cupcakes, 74
- Pink Lemonade Cupcakes, 50
- Raindrop Cupcakes, 40
- Snowy Owl Cupcakes, 118
- Sweet Snowflakes, 132
- White Chocolate Macadamia Cupcakes, 164

Cake Mix, Yellow
- Banana Cream Pie Cupcakes, 236
- Boston Cream Pie Minis, 226
- Caramel Apple Cupcakes, 102
- Chocolate Chip Cookie Cupcakes, 176
- Easter Chicks, 16
- Easy Easter Cupcakes, 44

Cake Mix, Yellow *(continued)*
Lazy Daisy Cupcakes, 18
Leprechaun Cupcakes, 24
Little Lamb Cakes, 40
Mini Doughnut Cupcakes, 104
Panda Cupcakes, 190
Peanut Butter & Jelly Cupcakes, 94
Pink Piglets, 212
Spider Web Pull-Apart Cake, 108
Tropical Luau Cupcakes, 64
Wigglin' Jigglin' Cupcakes, 116
Cannoli Cupcakes, 242
Cappuccino Cupcakes, 88
Caramel
Caramel Apple Cupcakes, 102
Caramel Frosting, 102
Caramel-Topped Cheesecakes with Oat-Pecan Crust, 238
Chocolate Caramel Bites, 166
Mini Praline Cakes, 222
Taffy Apple Cupcakes, 90
Caramel Apple Cupcakes, 102
Caramel Frosting, 102
Caramel-Topped Cheesecakes with Oat-Pecan Crust, 238
Carrot Cake Minis, 80
Carrots
Carrot Cake Minis, 80
Funny Bunnies, 34
Chai Latte Cupcakes, 144
Cheesecake
Caramel-Topped Cheesecakes with Oat-Pecan Crust, 238
Chocolate Cheesecakes for Two, 124
Creamy Strawberry Cookie "Tarts," 36
Filled Rich Chocolate Cupcakes, 182
Midnight Chocolate Cheesecake Cookie Cups, 162
Mini Lemon Cheesecakes, 230
Mini Oreo® Surprise Cupcakes, 156
No-Bake Mini Cheesecakes, 202
Petit Mocha Cheesecakes, 186
Toffee Bits Cheesecake Cups, 110
Cherry
Brownie Bon Bons, 234
Cherry Cupcakes, 48
Cherry Cupcakes, 48
Chocolate, 150–187
Black Cat Cupcakes, 86
Blue Suede Cupcakes, 206
Boston Cream Pie Minis, 226
Brownie Bon Bons, 234
Chocolate *(continued)*
Cappuccino Cupcakes, 88
Cherry Cupcakes, 48
Chocolate Cheesecakes for Two, 124
Chocolate Easter Baskets, 20
Chocolate Fudge Filling, 235
Chocolate Sweetheart Cupcakes, 118
Christmas Tree Cupcakes, 146
Cookies & Cream Cupcakes, 110
Cream-Filled Cupcakes, 194
Cubcakes, 196
Dinocakes, 204
Double Malted Cupcakes, 106
Feathered Friends, 100
Festive Chocolate Cupcakes, 138
Fortune Teller Cupcakes, 200
Friendly Ghost Cupcakes, 78
Graduation Party Cupcakes, 58
Halloween Hedgehogs, 92
Hot Chocolate Cupcakes, 128
Individual Flower Pot Cakes, 32
Magically Minty Mini Cupcakes, 36

Index

Chocolate *(continued)*
- Meteorite Mini Cakes, 208
- Mini Bees, 42
- Mini Fireworks, 48
- Mummy Cakes, 96
- No-Bake Mini Cheesecakes, 202
- Ooze Cupcakes, 198
- Panda Cupcakes, 190
- Patriotic Cocoa Cupcakes, 54
- Peanut Butter Cupcakes, 148
- Pecan Tassies, 98
- Peppermint Mocha Cupcakes, 142
- Pistachio-Chocolate Chip Cupcakes, 140
- Play Ball, 62
- Polka Dot Pumpkin Cupcakes, 86
- Red Velvet Cupcakes, 130
- Red's Rockin' Rainbow Cupcakes, 44
- S'more-Topped Cupcakes, 72
- Snowy Peaks, 114
- Spicy Chocolate Cupcakes, 228
- Spicy Chocolate Frosting, 228
- Whoopie Pie Cupcakes, 214
- Zebra Stripes, 208

Chocolate Buttercream Frosting, 170
Chocolate Caramel Bites, 166
Chocolate Cheesecakes for Two, 124
Chocolate Chip Cookie Cupcakes, 176
Chocolate Easter Baskets, 20
Chocolate Filling, 162
Chocolate Fudge Filling, 235
Chocolate Glaze, 186
Chocolate Hazelnut Cupcakes, 158
Chocolate Moose, 160
Chocolate Sweetheart Cupcakes, 118
Chocolate Tiramisu Cupcakes, 184

Christmas
- Christmas Tree Cupcakes, 146
- Festive Chocolate Cupcakes, 138
- Holiday Poke Cupcakes, 132
- Mini Fruitcake Cupcakes, 126
- Sweet Snowmen, 122
- Wigglin' Jigglin' Cupcakes, 116

Christmas Tree Cupcakes, 146
Classic Chocolate Cupcakes, 170

Coconut
- Firecracker Cupcakes, 66
- German Chocolate Cupcakes, 180
- Scarecrow Cupcakes, 82
- Snowy Owl Cupcakes, 118
- Sweet Snowmen, 122
- Tropical Luau Cupcakes, 64

Coffee
- Cappuccino Cupcakes, 88
- Chocolate Tiramisu Cupcakes, 184
- Coffee Brownie Bites, 164
- Iced Coffee Cupcakes, 152
- Mocha Glaze, 178
- Peppermint Mocha Cupcakes, 142
- Petit Mocha Cheesecakes, 186

Coffee Brownie Bites, 164
Colorful Caterpillar Cupcakes, 52
Colossal Birthday Cupcake, 214
Cookies & Cream Cupcakes, 110
Cranberries: Glazed Cranberry Mini-Cakes, 136
Cream Cheese Frosting, 80, 112
Cream Cheese Surprise Cupcakes, 168
Cream-Filled Cupcakes, 194
Creamy Strawberry Cookie "Tarts," 36
Crumb Crust, 186
Cubcakes, 196

Dark Chocolate Banana Cupcakes, 150
Dinocakes, 204
Double Malted Cupcakes, 106
Dragonflies, 46

E

Easter
Chocolate Easter Baskets, 20
Easter Chicks, 16
Easy Easter Cupcakes, 44
Funny Bunnies, 34
Little Lamb Cakes, 40
Easter Chicks, 16
Easy Easter Cupcakes, 44

F

Feathered Friends, 100
Festive Chocolate Cupcakes, 138
Filled Rich Chocolate Cupcakes, 182
Filling, 182
Firecracker Cupcakes, 66
Fishy Friends, 196
Fortune Teller Cupcakes, 200
Fourth of July
All-American Cupcakes, 66
Firecracker Cupcakes, 66
Mini Fireworks, 48
Patriotic Cocoa Cupcakes, 54
Friendly Frogs, 30
Friendly Ghost Cupcakes, 78
Frostings and Glazes
Apple Cider Frosting, 76
Apple Glaze, 84
Browned Butter Frosting, 134
Buttercream Frosting, 146
Caramel Frosting, 102
Frostings and Glazes *(continued)*
Chocolate Buttercream Frosting, 170
Chocolate Glaze, 186
Cream Cheese Frosting, 80, 112
Mocha Glaze, 178
Peanut Buttery Frosting, 148
Simple Fall Frosting, 82
Spicy Chocolate Frosting, 228
Vanilla Frosting, 54
White Glaze, 136
Funny Bunnies, 34

G

Gelatin
Creamy Strawberry Cookie "Tarts," 36
Holiday Poke Cupcakes, 132
Lovin' Sweetcakes, 142
Raindrop Cupcakes, 40
Wigglin' Jigglin' Cupcakes, 116
German Chocolate Cupcakes, 180
Glazed Applesauce Spice Cakes, 84
Glazed Cranberry Mini-Cakes, 136
Goblin's Delight Filling, 182
Graduation Party Cupcakes, 58
Grape Soda Cupcakes, 188
Graveyard Cupcakes, 104
Gumdrop Hats, 82

H

Halloween
Black Cat Cupcakes, 86
Friendly Ghost Cupcakes, 78
Goblin's Delight Filling, 182
Graveyard Cupcakes, 104
Halloween Hedgehogs, 92
Mummy Cakes, 96
Ooze Cupcakes, 198
Scarecrow Cupcakes, 82
Spider Web Pull-Apart Cake, 108
Taffy Apple Cupcakes, 90
Halloween Hedgehogs, 92
Hidden Berry Cupcakes, 60
Holiday Poke Cupcakes, 132
Holidays *(see individual listings)*
Hot Chocolate Cupcakes, 128

I

I Think You're "Marbleous" Cupcakes, 124
Ice Cream: Iced Coffee Cupcakes, 152
Ice Cream Cone Cupcakes, 58
Iced Coffee Cupcakes, 152
Individual Flower Pot Cakes, 32

Index

I

Jelly Doughnut Bites, 240

Jumbo Muffin Pan

- Lemon Meringue Cupcakes, 38
- Molton Cinnamon-Chocolate Cakes, 176
- Snowy Peaks, 114

K

Key Lime Pie Cupcakes, 18

Kids' Favorites

- Blue Suede Cupcakes, 206
- Chocolate Chip Cookie Cupcakes, 176
- Chocolate Moose, 160
- Classic Chocolate Cupcakes, 170
- Colorful Caterpillar Cupcakes, 52
- Colossal Birthday Cupcake, 214
- Cookies & Cream Cupcakes, 110
- Cream-Filled Cupcakes, 194
- Cubcakes, 196
- Dinocakes, 204
- Dragonflies, 46
- Fishy Friends, 196
- Fortune Teller Cupcakes, 200
- Friendly Frogs, 30
- Funny Bunnies, 34
- Grape Soda Cupcakes, 188

Kids' Favorites *(continued)*

- Ice Cream Cone Cupcakes, 58
- Individual Flower Pot Cakes, 32
- Jelly Doughnut Bites, 240
- Lazy Daisy Cupcakes, 18
- Little Lamb Cakes, 40
- Marshmallow Delights, 26
- Meteorite Mini Cakes, 208
- Mini Bees, 42
- Mini Oreo® Surprise Cupcakes, 156
- Monkey A-Rounds, 174
- Ooze Cupcakes, 198
- Orange Dreamsicle Cupcakes, 218
- Panda Cupcakes, 190
- Pink Lemonade Cupcakes, 50
- Pink Piglets, 212
- Play Ball, 62
- Pupcakes, 192
- Raindrop Cupcakes, 40
- Red's Rockin' Rainbow Cupcakes, 44
- Rocky Road Cupcakes, 168
- S'more-Topped Cupcakes, 72
- Strawberry Milkshake Cupcakes, 22
- Triple Chocolate PB Minis, 172
- Under the Sea, 68
- Whoopie Pie Cupcakes, 214
- Wigglin' Jigglin' Cupcakes, 116

L

Lazy Daisy Cupcakes, 18

Lemon

- Lemon Blueberry Shortcakes, 244
- Lemon-Cream Cheese Cupcakes, 28
- Lemon Meringue Cupcakes, 38
- Lemon Poppy Seed Cupcakes, 244
- Limoncello Cupcakes, 220
- Mini Lemon Cheesecakes, 230
- Pink Lemonade Cupcakes, 50

Lemon Blueberry Shortcakes, 244

Lemon-Cream Cheese Cupcakes, 28

Lemon Meringue Cupcakes, 38

Lemon Poppy Seed Cupcakes, 244

Leopard Spots, 192

Leprechaun Cupcakes, 24

Lime

- Key Lime Pie Cupcakes, 18
- Margarita Cupcakes, 74
- Ooze Cupcakes, 198

Limoncello Cupcakes, 220

Liquor

- Cappuccino Cupcakes, 88
- Limoncello Cupcakes, 220
- Margarita Cupcakes, 74
- Mini Fruitcake Cupcakes, 126

Little Lamb Cakes, 40
Lovin' Sweetcakes, 142

M

Macadamia Nuts: White Chocolate Macadamia Cupcakes, 164
Magically Minty Mini Cupcakes, 36
Maple Bacon Cupcakes, 232
Margarita Cupcakes, 74
Marshmallow Delights, 26
Marshmallow
- Easy Easter Cupcakes, 44
- Funny Bunnies, 34
- Lazy Daisy Cupcakes, 18
- Little Lamb Cakes, 40
- Marshmallow Delights, 26
- Pistachio-Chocolate Chip Cupcakes, 140
- Rocky Road Cupcakes, 168
- S'more-Topped Cupcakes, 72
- Sweet Little Sheep, 216
- Sweet Snowmen, 122

Meteorite Mini Cakes, 208
Midnight Chocolate Cheesecake Cookie Cups, 162
Mini Bees, 42
Mini Brownie Cups, 178
Mini Doughnut Cupcakes, 104
Mini Fireworks, 48
Mini Fruitcake Cupcakes, 126
Mini Lemon Cheesecakes, 230
Mini Muffin Pan
- Brownie Bon Bons, 234
- Carrot Cake Minis, 80
- Chocolate Caramel Bites, 166
- Coffee Brownie Bites, 164
- Easter Chicks, 16
- Glazed Cranberry Mini-Cakes, 136
- Jelly Doughnut Bites, 240
- Magically Minty Mini Cupcakes, 36
- Midnight Chocolate Cheesecake Cookie Cups, 162
- Mini Bees, 42
- Mini Brownie Cups, 178
- Mini Doughnut Cupcakes, 104
- Mini Fruitcake Cupcakes, 126
- Pecan Tassies, 98
- Pink Piglets, 212
- Quick Cookie Cupcakes, 158
- Sweet Little Sheep, 216
- Taffy Apple Cupcakes, 90
- Tangy Raspberry Minis, 56
- Triple Chocolate PB Minis, 172
- Truffle Brownie Bites, 154
- Zesty Orange Cookie Cups, 120

Mini Oreo® Surprise Cupcakes, 156
Mini Praline Cakes, 222
Mint
- Christmas Tree Cupcakes, 146
- Magically Minty Mini Cupcakes, 36
- Peppermint Mocha Cupcakes, 142

Mocha Glaze, 178
Molton Cinnamon-Chocolate Cakes, 176
Monkey A-Rounds, 174
Mummy Cakes, 96

N

No-Bake Mini Cheesecakes, 202
Nuts *(see individual listings)*

O

Oats
- Caramel-Topped Cheesecakes with Oat-Pecan Crust, 238
- Hidden Berry Cupcakes, 60

Ooze Cupcakes, 198
Orange
- Cannoli Cupcakes, 242
- Colorful Caterpillar Cupcakes, 52
- Mini Fruitcake Cupcakes, 126
- Orange Dreamsicle Cupcakes, 218
- Zesty Orange Cookie Cups, 120

Orange Dreamsicle Cupcakes, 218

Index

P

Panda Cupcakes, 190
Patriotic Cocoa Cupcakes, 54
Peanut Butter
- Chocolate Chip Cookie Cupcakes, 176
- Colossal Birthday Cupcake, 214
- Peanut Butter & Jelly Cupcakes, 94
- Peanut Butter Cupcakes, 148
- Peanut Buttery Frosting, 148
- Triple Chocolate PB Minis, 172

Peanut Butter & Jelly Cupcakes, 94
Peanut Butter Cupcakes, 148
Peanut Buttery Frosting, 148
Peanuts: Taffy Apple Cupcakes, 90
Pecan Tassies, 98
Pecans
- Butter Pecan Cupcakes, 134
- Caramel Apple Cupcakes, 102
- Caramel-Topped Cheesecakes with Oat-Pecan Crust, 238
- German Chocolate Cupcakes, 180
- Iced Coffee Cupcakes, 152

Pecans *(continued)*
- Mini Fruitcake Cupcakes, 126
- Mini Praline Cakes, 222
- Pecan Tassies, 98
- Touchdown Brownie Cups, 92

Peppermint Mocha Cupcakes, 142
Petit Mocha Cheesecakes, 186
Pineapple: Tropical Luau Cupcakes, 64
Pink Lemonade Cupcakes, 50
Pink Piglets, 212
Pistachio-Chocolate Chip Cupcakes, 140
Pistachios: Pistachio-Chocolate Chip Cupcakes, 140
Play Ball, 62
Polka Dot Pumpkin Cupcakes, 86
Pudding Mix
- Banana Cream Pie Cupcakes, 236
- Boston Cream Pie Minis, 226
- Iced Coffee Cupcakes, 152
- Lemon-Cream Cheese Cupcakes, 28
- Limoncello Cupcakes, 220
- Tropical Luau Cupcakes, 64
- White Chocolate Macadamia Cupcakes, 164

Pumpkin: Polka Dot Pumpkin Cupcakes, 86
Pupcakes, 192

Q

Quick Cookie Cupcakes, 158

R

Raindrop Cupcakes, 40
Raspberry
- Chocolate Sweetheart Cupcakes, 118
- Jelly Doughnut Bites, 240
- Tangy Raspberry Minis, 56

Red Velvet Cupcakes, 130
Red's Rockin' Rainbow Cupcakes, 44
Rocky Road Cupcakes, 168

S

Scarecrow Cupcakes, 82
Simple Fall Frosting, 82
S'more-Topped Cupcakes, 72
Snowy Owl Cupcakes, 118
Snowy Peaks, 114
Spicy Chocolate Cupcakes, 228
Spicy Chocolate Frosting, 228
Spider Web Pull-Apart Cake, 108
St. Patrick's Day
- Leprechaun Cupcakes, 24
- Magically Minty Mini Cupcakes, 36

Strawberry
Creamy Strawberry Cookie "Tarts," 36
Hidden Berry Cupcakes, 60
Peanut Butter & Jelly Cupcakes, 94
Strawberry Milkshake Cupcakes, 22
Strawberry Preserve Cupcakes, 70
Strawberry Milkshake Cupcakes, 22
Strawberry Preserve Cupcakes, 70
Sunny Side Upcakes, 202
Sweet Little Sheep, 216
Sweet Potato Spice Cupcakes, 112
Sweet Snowflakes, 132
Sweet Snowmen, 122

T

Taffy Apple Cupcakes, 90
Tangy Raspberry Minis, 56
Tea: Chai Latte Cupcakes, 144
Thanksgiving: Feathered Friends, 100
Toffee Bits Cheesecake Cups, 110
Touchdown Brownie Cups, 92
Triple Chocolate PB Minis, 172
Tropical Luau Cupcakes, 64
Truffle Brownie Bites, 154

U

Under the Sea, 68

V

Valentine Filling, 182
Valentine's Day
Chocolate Cheesecakes for Two, 124
Chocolate Sweetheart Cupcakes, 118
I Think You're "Marbleous" Cupcakes, 124
Lovin' Sweetcakes, 142
Red Velvet Cupcakes, 130
Valentine Filling, 182
Vanilla Frosting, 54

W

Walnuts
Apple Cider Cupcakes, 76
Chocolate Chip Cookie Cupcakes, 176
Glazed Applesauce Spice Cakes, 84
Glazed Cranberry Mini-Cakes, 136
Rocky Road Cupcakes, 168
Sweet Potato Spice Cupcakes, 112
White Chocolate (*see also* **Almond Bark**)
Glazed Cranberry Mini-Cakes, 136
White Chocolate Macadamia Cupcakes, 164
White Glaze, 136
Zebra Stripes, 208
Zesty Orange Cookie Cups, 120
White Chocolate Macadamia Cupcakes, 164
White Glaze, 136
Whoopie Pie Cupcakes, 214
Wigglin' Jigglin' Cupcakes, 116

Z

Zebra Stripes, 208
Zesty Orange Cookie Cups, 120

Metric Conversion Chart

VOLUME MEASUREMENTS (dry)

1/8 teaspoon = 0.5 mL
1/4 teaspoon = 1 mL
1/2 teaspoon = 2 mL
3/4 teaspoon = 4 mL
1 teaspoon = 5 mL
1 tablespoon = 15 mL
2 tablespoons = 30 mL
1/4 cup = 60 mL
1/3 cup = 75 mL
1/2 cup = 125 mL
2/3 cup = 150 mL
3/4 cup = 175 mL
1 cup = 250 mL
2 cups = 1 pint = 500 mL
3 cups = 750 mL
4 cups = 1 quart = 1 L

VOLUME MEASUREMENTS (fluid)

1 fluid ounce (2 tablespoons) = 30 mL
4 fluid ounces (1/2 cup) = 125 mL
8 fluid ounces (1 cup) = 250 mL
12 fluid ounces (1 1/2 cups) = 375 mL
16 fluid ounces (2 cups) = 500 mL

WEIGHTS (mass)

1/2 ounce = 15 g
1 ounce = 30 g
3 ounces = 90 g
4 ounces = 120 g
8 ounces = 225 g
10 ounces = 285 g
12 ounces = 360 g
16 ounces = 1 pound = 450 g

DIMENSIONS

1/16 inch = 2 mm
1/8 inch = 3 mm
1/4 inch = 6 mm
1/2 inch = 1.5 cm
3/4 inch = 2 cm
1 inch = 2.5 cm

OVEN TEMPERATURES

250°F = 120°C
275°F = 140°C
300°F = 150°C
325°F = 160°C
350°F = 180°C
375°F = 190°C
400°F = 200°C
425°F = 220°C
450°F = 230°C

BAKING PAN SIZES

Utensil	Size in Inches/Quarts	Metric Volume	Size in Centimeters
Baking or Cake Pan (square or rectangular)	8×8×2	2 L	20×20×5
	9×9×2	2.5 L	23×23×5
	12×8×2	3 L	30×20×5
	13×9×2	3.5 L	33×23×5
Loaf Pan	8×4×3	1.5 L	20×10×7
	9×5×3	2 L	23×13×7
Round Layer Cake Pan	8×1½	1.2 L	20×4
	9×1½	1.5 L	23×4
Pie Plate	8×1¼	750 mL	20×3
	9×1¼	1 L	23×3
Baking Dish or Casserole	1 quart	1 L	—
	1½ quart	1.5 L	—
	2 quart	2 L	—